Why Shadow Banking Didn't Cause the Financial Crisis—and Why Regulating Contagion Won't Help

by Norbert J. Michel

ISBN: 978-1-952223-47-1
eBook ISBN: 978-1-952223-48-8

Printed in the United States of America

Cover design: Faceout Studio, Spencer Fuller

Cato Institute
1000 Massachusetts Ave. NW
Washington, DC 20001
www.cato.org

TABLE OF CONTENTS

ABBREVIATIONS AND ACRONYMS

ABCP	asset-backed commercial paper
ABS	asset-backed security
AIG	American International Group
AMLF	ABCP money market mutual fund liquidity facility
BIS	Bank for International Settlements
CDO	collateralized debt obligation
CDS	credit default swap
CPFF	Commercial Paper Funding Facility
DGP	Debt Guarantee Program
FASB	Financial Accounting Standards Board
FDIC	Federal Deposit Insurance Corporation
FHLB	Federal Home Loan Bank
FSOC	Financial Stability Oversight Council
GAO	U.S. Government Accountability Office
GDP	gross domestic product
GSE	government-sponsored enterprise
IOLTA	Interest on Lawyers' Trust Account
LIBOR-OIS spread	difference between London Interbank Offered Rate and the overnight index swap
MBS	mortgage-backed security
MMF	money market mutual fund
MMLF	MMF Liquidity Facility
NAV	net asset value
NOW	negotiable order of withdrawal
OCC	Office of the Comptroller of the Currency
PDCF	Primary Dealer Credit Facility

INTRODUCTION

The following is a common description of the 2008 financial crisis: unregulated Wall Street firms (shadow banks) made excessively risky bets with derivatives, and then the housing bubble burst. Panic ensued, and it nearly destroyed the financial system, but the federal government stepped in and prevented another Great Depression. The traditional banking sector, however, was highly regulated and unable to take so many risky bets. The way to guard against future crises, therefore, is to regulate shadow banks more like commercial banks and to federally back their securities as if they were retail bank deposits.

This story has many variations, often including Lehman Brothers' bankruptcy and the run on the Reserve Primary Fund, a large money market mutual fund (MMF), but its core remains the conventional view of the 2008 crisis in most academic and policy circles, especially in Washington, DC. Countless government officials used this story to justify both their actions during the crisis and the major regulatory changes they implemented afterward. Now, Biden administration officials are using this story to promote more regulations for MMFs, a key part of the supposedly dangerous shadow banking system, and even to justify allowing only federally insured banks to issue stablecoins, a type of cryptocurrency that did not exist in 2008.

Yet the record demonstrates that the core of this story—that unregulated shadow banks, rather than highly regulated traditional banks, nearly caused another Great Depression because they made so many risky bets unbeknownst to federal regulators—is at best highly misleading. In fact, bank regulators blessed much of the shadow banking activity because it took place in the traditional banking sector. Moreover, while supporters of the conventional story liken the 2008 runs on shadow banks to the indiscriminate bank depositor runs experienced in the United States prior to federal deposit insurance, the evidence for such random behavior is surprisingly scarce. Moreover, most of the evidence suggests that instead of investment flows being due to contagion, investors made carefully targeted moves to improve their positions, often because of regulatory or legal requirements.

There is good reason, for instance, to doubt that contagion from indiscriminate panic caused the run on the Reserve Primary Fund to spread to the rest of the MMF sector or that it caused turmoil to spread from MMFs to the rest of short-term credit markets. There is even good reason to doubt that federal involvement in credit markets stopped the 2008 crisis or that strictly regulating more financial firms would result in greater financial stability. This book provides a comprehensive account of the conventional 2008 crisis story and demonstrates that it does not provide a solid foundation for spreading more banklike regulations to the rest of the financial markets.

1

THE SHADOW BANKS REVEALED

In the wake of the 2008 financial crisis, proponents of stricter regulation insisted that firms in the shadow banking sector were the main drivers of the turmoil. The term *shadow banking,* apparently coined by economist Paul McCulley in 2007, is typically used to describe financial firms in capital markets rather than depository institutions in the commercial banking sector.[1] For instance, a 2010 Brookings Institution research paper states that in "its broadest definition, shadow banking includes such familiar institutions as investment banks, money-market mutual funds, and mortgage brokers; some rather old contractual forms, such as sale-and-repurchase agreements (repos); and more esoteric instruments such as asset-backed securities (ABSs), collateralized debt obligations (CDOs), and asset-backed commercial paper (ABCP)."[2]

Many government officials have used this term to explain what happened during the 2008 crisis. For example, in 2015, then–Federal Reserve chair Janet Yellen gave a speech that included the following passage:

> The crisis had many causes, including the numerous factors that drove a lengthy housing boom and the expansion of a largely unregulated "shadow banking system"

rivaling the traditional banking sector in size. A self-reinforcing financial panic magnified the damage from risks that had built up over many years throughout the country and across the financial system.[3]

During the crisis, Yellen was president of the Federal Reserve Bank of San Francisco, and her remarks are wholly consistent with those of 2008 Federal Reserve chair Ben Bernanke. In 2010, Bernanke's statement to the Financial Crisis Inquiry Commission read as follows:

> Shadow banks are financial entities other than regulated depository institutions (commercial banks, thrifts, and credit unions) that serve as intermediaries to channel savings into investment. . . . As was illustrated by the ABCP market meltdown . . . the reliance of shadow banks on short-term uninsured funds made them subject to runs, much as commercial banks and thrift institutions had been exposed to runs prior to the creation of deposit insurance. . . . When short-term wholesale funding markets came under stress, particularly in the period after the collapse of Lehman Brothers, money market mutual funds faced runs by their investors. Although actions by the Treasury and the Federal Reserve helped arrest these runs, the money market mutual funds responded by hoarding liquidity, thus constricting the availability of financing to financial and nonfinancial firms. Critically, shadow banks were, for the most part, not subject to consistent and effective regulatory oversight.[4]

Timothy Geithner, who was serving as president of the Federal Reserve Bank of New York during 2008 and whom President Obama later named U.S. Treasury Secretary, released a book in 2014 that tells his own version of what happened during the crisis. As treasury secretary, Geithner was instrumental in pushing new MMF regulations forward. His book states:

> The Reserve Fund debacle discouraged risk taking by other money funds, which meant even less buying of commercial paper and less lending through repo, which meant an even more intense liquidity crisis for banks and other institutions. Basically, short-term financing—whether secured by collateral or not—was vanishing. No collateral, no matter how safe historically, was viewed as truly liquid, because there was simply no liquidity in the system to buy it. This would have been the textbook definition of a panic, except no textbook had recorded anything like it.[5]

MMFs are one of the few nonbank intermediaries from the shadow banking system that ultimately had to comply with major new federal regulations after the 2008 crisis, and Geithner played a role in building support for those changes. Later in his book, when lamenting that the Securities and Exchange Commission (SEC) had not yet implemented a new round of MMF reforms, Geithner discusses how "the instability of money market funds contributed to the worst financial crisis since the Great Depression."[6]

This basic story about the 2008 financial crisis is commonly retold in policy papers, scholarly books, and popular accounts of the crisis. For example, in his best-selling book, *Too Big to Fail: The Inside Story of How Wall Street and Washington Fought to Save the Financial System—and Themselves,* Andrew Ross Sorkin tells the story of how U.S. Treasury Secretary Hank Paulson, looking at his Bloomberg terminal for updates on the Reserve Primary Fund, suddenly recognized that the MMF's troubles were "starting to spread throughout the rest of the field."[7] Sorkin then says that the "Lehman-induced panic was spreading like a plague, the black death of Wall Street," and Paulson recognized that the "money market industry needed to be shored up."[8]

In the introduction to his book, Vanderbilt Law School professor (and former Treasury senior policy adviser from 2009 to 2010) Morgan Ricks explains that "the concept of shadow banking . . . is more or less interchangeable with the (nondeposit) short-term debt of the financial sector"[9] and that during 2007 and 2008, these shadow banking markets "unraveled in a series of classic panics."[10] Ricks argues that "from the perspective of finance practitioners and policy-makers, these panics were virtually synonymous with the financial crisis."[11] Similarly, a report by the Center for American Progress states that "shadow banks helped spark the 2007–08 crisis by originating subprime mortgages, packaging them into mortgage-backed securities, and distributing them throughout the financial system. They also exacerbated the crisis when creditors ran from the shadow banking sector, similar to old-fashioned depositor runs."[12]

On its website, the Corporate Finance Institute, an online training platform for finance professionals, states:

> The shadow banking industry is viewed as heavily contributing to the housing market collapse and the world-wide financial crisis that began in 2008. . . . It occurred in part because shadow banking companies are not subject to the same regulations—such as reserve requirements—that regular commercial banks are constrained by. . . . They are able to operate with higher levels of liquidity risk and credit risk compared to traditional bank lenders.[13]

The personal finance website The Balance puts the story in very stark terms:

> Investors knew that Lehman's bankruptcy threatened the financial institutions that owned its bonds. . . .

On September 17, 2008, the collapse spread. Investors withdrew a record $196 billion from their money market accounts. If the run had continued, businesses wouldn't have been able to get money to fund their day-to-day operations. In just a few weeks, the economy would have collapsed.[14]

Finally, the story is also commonly repeated in official government reports and even federal agencies' formal rule proposals. In December 2020, the President's Working Group on Financial Markets (PWG) released a report on "reform options" for MMFs that includes the following passage:

> In September 2008, there was a run on certain types of MMFs after the failure of Lehman Brothers caused a large prime MMF that held Lehman Brothers short-term instruments to sustain losses and "break the buck." [The share price fell below $1.] During that time, prime MMFs experienced significant redemptions that contributed to dislocations in short-term funding markets, while government MMFs experienced net inflows. Ultimately, the run on prime MMFs abated after announcements of a Treasury guarantee program for MMFs and a Federal Reserve facility designed to provide liquidity to MMFs. Subsequently, the Securities and Exchange Commission ("SEC") adopted reforms (in 2010 and 2014) that were designed to address the structural vulnerabilities that became apparent in 2008.[15]

In December 2021, the Biden administration's SEC released a formal rule proposal for MMFs. The proposal tells the familiar tale as follows:

> For example, during 2007–2008, some prime money market funds were exposed to substantial losses from certain of their holdings. At that time, one money market fund "broke the buck" and suspended redemptions,

and many fund sponsors provided financial support to their funds. These events, along with general turbulence in the financial markets, led to a run primarily on institutional prime money market funds and contributed to severe dislocations in short-term credit markets. The U.S. Department of the Treasury and the Board of Governors of the Federal Reserve System subsequently announced intervention in the short-term markets that was effective in containing the run on prime money market funds and providing additional liquidity to money market funds.[16]

These severe "dislocations in short-term credit markets" are, of course, a main justification for the systemic risk regulations implemented after the 2008 financial crisis.

Much of the post-2008 regulatory effort, however, was concentrated in the traditional banking sector, not in the shadow banking sector—a fact that warrants skepticism toward the conventional story of the 2008 crisis. Yet MMFs were also singled out for multiple new regulations during that period. As the new SEC rule proposal makes clear, MMFs are once again being singled out for essentially the same reasons. According to the new proposal, "Early redemptions can deplete a fund's daily or weekly liquid assets, which reduces liquidity of the remainder of the fund's portfolio and increases the risk that a fund may need to sell less liquid assets into the market during fire sales."[17] Ostensibly, the goal of the newly proposed rule is to reduce shareholders' incentives to redeem their shares.

There is much to evaluate in the conventional story of the 2008 financial crisis, especially regarding the instruments that have made the shadow banking industry infamous. These instruments range from repos and a variety of securitized assets to intermediaries such as MMFs and securities dealers. To begin that evaluation, the following is a brief overview of the main financing mechanisms and how they fit into the financial sector.

Commercial Paper and Asset-Backed Commercial Paper

The U.S. commercial paper market has existed since the early 1800s and has consistently been a source of nonbank credit for large companies.[18] Commercial paper is a short-term debt instrument that firms (financial and nonfinancial) issue to finance their short-term needs, such as payroll, receivables, and inventory. Most commercial paper is issued only by very large companies with stellar credit ratings, such as Ford, John Deere, and Citigroup.[19] It is issued in large denominations (at least $100,000), and it matures on a specific date. Although the term can be as long as 270 days, most commercial paper matures in less than one week.[20] Generally, only large institutional investors (such as private pension funds, commercial and investment banks, and mutual funds) can buy commercial paper, so most retail consumers have access to these investments only through an intermediary, such as an MMF. Regardless of the type of intermediary, these institutional investors provide firms with cash. In other words, firms that issue commercial paper borrow money from large institutional investors. Many of those institutional investors have a cash surplus, so the commercial paper market serves as a low-risk investment/cash management opportunity. Typically, commercial paper is issued at a discount from face value, meaning that a buyer pays less than face value and then receives the full face value at maturity; the difference is the buyer's profit. The commercial paper market is highly liquid, with very short-term maturities, so it is common for issuers to roll over their commercial paper, meaning that they constantly issue new paper (borrow more) to pay off their maturing issues. Traditionally, commercial paper was unsecured debt. However, *asset-backed* commercial paper (ABCP) is secured debt, typically backed by specific assets (such as auto loans, home mortgages, credit card debt, or some combination) that serve as collateral. Though ABCP has typically been more expensive than traditional commercial paper, companies use both types as a low-cost alternative to bank debt. Normally, commercial banks set up special entities (conduits) to issue ABCP and provide credit or liquidity guarantees. In other words, most ABCP is sold to outside investors with explicit guarantees that require commercial banks to pay off maturing ABCP at full face value in the event of default.[21] As of June 2020, the total U.S. commercial paper outstanding was just over $1 trillion, roughly half as much as the all-time high reached in July 2007.[22] The decline from 2007 is attributable almost entirely to a reduction in the amount of ABCP issued after the drop in value during the crisis. Incidentally, the amount of ABCP issued increased dramatically in 2005, and it has never returned to even the levels outstanding before 2005.[23]

Repo Agreements

Repo agreements have existed in the United States since at least 1917, when the Federal Reserve used them to extend credit to member banks.[24] They are debt instruments where one party agrees to sell securities, often Treasury securities, for cash and to repurchase those same securities later (usually the next day) at a higher price. Thus, a repo is a collateralized short-term loan: one party borrows cash from another and provides securities for collateral. If the borrower fails to repurchase the securities as promised, the lender simply

keeps the securities. Generally, the borrower overcollateral-
izes the loan by borrowing less than the value of the securities. By posting, for example, $1,000,000 in Treasuries as
collateral, a firm could borrow $985,0000. (The profit in
this example would be expressed as a 1.5 percent *haircut*.)
The Federal Reserve has engaged in repo transactions since
its inception, but until 2013, it did so mainly as a lender of
cash to its primary dealers in the conduct of its normal monetary policy (open market) operations.[25] Repos allow firms
with large pools of cash to earn interest on their funds while
providing borrowers with an inexpensive, low-risk alternative to bank loans for short-term financing. Repos can be
for terms of up to two years, but most are issued on an overnight basis.[26] U.S. Treasury securities are by far the most
commonly used collateral in the repo market, with agency
debt and mortgage-backed securities (MBSs) a close second,
such that approximately 70 percent of the collateral used
in the repo market consists of government-backed securities.[27] As with commercial paper, it is common for issuers
to roll over their borrowings, meaning that they constantly
issue new repos to pay off maturing issues. The denominations are typically very large (millions of dollars), and only
large corporations, commercial banks, securities dealers,
and other institutional investors, such as mutual funds, are
involved in the repo market.[28] Historically, securities dealers
have been the largest borrowers in the repo markets, with
an average share of more than 53 percent of total borrowings for the past 20 years, *and* the largest investors in the
repo market, accounting for 40 percent of the total share for
the past 20 years.[29] In other words, dealers usually exchange
both cash and securities in the repo market for their clients,
so much so that the dealers are the largest participants in
the market. The two major segments of the repo market are

the tri-party repo market, in which a clearing bank (either the Bank of New York Mellon or JPMorgan Chase) provides settlement and collateral management services, and the bilateral repo market, in which all repos are executed directly by the counterparties (the borrowers and lenders).[30]

Money Market Mutual Funds

MMFs, introduced in 1971,[31] are just one of the many types of mutual funds—that is, intermediaries that pool investors' funds to buy a portfolio of investments. MMFs issue shares so that investors can use their own money to buy shares of the portfolio. Put differently, investors always own a proportionate share of an MMF's asset portfolio, so a fund cannot "run out" of shares to return to its investors even if the share value falls. MMFs pool investors' money to purchase only short-term (money market) instruments, such as Treasury securities, large-denomination certificates of deposit, commercial paper, and repos.[32] Most of these securities, of course, are federally backed, collateralized by federally backed securities, or guaranteed by banks that are federally insured. While some MMFs cater to institutional investors, others offer smaller retail customers investment opportunities that they otherwise would not have. Government MMFs invest mainly in government securities, tax-exempt MMFs invest mostly in state and local government debt securities, and prime MMFs invest in a broader range of money market instruments. While MMFs held almost half of outstanding commercial paper in the early 2000s, their investments in commercial paper have fallen in recent years, and they accounted for just 22 percent of the amount outstanding in June 2020 (a lower share, in fact, than that of nonfinancial firms).[33] In 2020, MMFs accounted for 22 percent of all repo lending,[34] but MMFs do not borrow in the repo market. That is, MMFs invest their shareholders' cash by lending in the repo market, just as other firms invest their cash. According to the SEC, approximately 70 percent of MMF repos either are for overnight maturities or can be terminated at any time, and another 24 percent have maturities between 1 and 7 days.[35] Unsurprisingly, because of their high liquidity and low risk, government securities have historically accounted for "the great majority of MMF repo collateral," with 64 and 31 percent collateralized by Treasuries and agency securities, respectively, as of December 2020.[36] Most MMF repos are executed in the tri-party repo market, and most MMFs invest their cash in repos with the financial institutions that serve as the Fed's primary dealers.[37] Because MMFs invest in highly liquid short-term securities, they typically offer investors limited check-writing privileges similar to those offered by commercial banks on deposit accounts.[38] An increasing number of commercial banks have sponsored MMFs since the 1980s. Bank-sponsored prime institutional MMFs, for instance, grew from "a negligible percentage of the industry in 1986" to almost half ($227 billion) of all prime institutional MMF assets by 2000 and further increased to 52 percent ($612 billion) by the end of 2007.[39] As with commercial paper, banks provide explicit guarantees for their conduits that create MMFs, thus increasing the liabilities for the commercial banking sector.[40]

Asset Securitization

Although it can be complex and detail laden, the process of securitizing assets is nothing more than forming groups (pools) of assets, such as mortgages, consumer loans, or other financial assets, and then creating securities tied to those assets. The general idea is that by aggregating multiple financial assets and packaging them into different securities with distinct maturities and risk characteristics, they will appeal to a wide array of investors with diverse needs. Some such securities are designed to be very low risk, and others are not. Before the 1980s, securitization was essentially done using only mortgages as the underlying assets, largely through the government-sponsored enterprise (GSE) Fannie Mae. Then, in 1985, Sperry Corporation sold $200 million in securities backed by a pool of leases on computer equipment, thus opening a floodgate of new securitizations.[41] After that sale, financial intermediaries rapidly increased their reliance on securitization using all sorts of financial assets. According to the Federal Reserve's flow of funds data, the liabilities of asset-backed security issuers "grew at a compound annual rate of forty-six percent from 1982 to 1999, and the non-mortgage segment of those issues grew at a compound annual rate of fifty-five percent."[42] From the very beginning, both nonbanks and commercial banks were heavily involved in asset securitization, and federal regulators were aware of banks' involvement. As the *New York Times* reported in 1985, Sperry, through its newly created security-issuing subsidiary, Sperry Lease Finance, registered its securities with the SEC and supported its securitization with an irrevocable bank letter of credit.[43] In 2012, a Federal Reserve report affirmed that "banks are by far the predominant force in the securitization market" and that banks were "a significant force in these shadow banking segments related to securitization all along."[44] From 1990 to 2008, commercial banks' market share for the principal functions of securitization (including issuing, trustee services, underwriting, and servicing) remained well over 90 percent.[45]

This overview demonstrates that repos and commercial paper are designed to provide a higher return than investors would expect from the safest investments, such as insured bank certificates of deposit and Treasuries, yet with very little risk compared to other capital market alternatives, such as equity securities. Similarly, MMFs are an intermediary that puts funds in only low-risk, liquid, short-term investments to provide a slightly higher return than what is available from making only the safest investments. Other than through MMFs, only the largest corporations (especially financial firms) and investors interact in these capital markets.

The summary also demonstrates that these investment vehicles—even the securitization process itself—existed long before the 2008 financial crisis. Moreover, referring to them as part of a shadow banking system is misleading because commercial banks have been heavily involved with commercial paper, repos, securitization, and MMFs for many years. None of this activity took place in the shadows, and almost all of it took place either directly through a commercial bank or through an affiliate of a (Federal Reserve–regulated) bank-holding company. It unequivocally occurred in the purview—indeed, with the explicit blessing—of banking regulators.[46]

More broadly, the term *shadow banking* can be misleading when it is used to liken all short-term capital market activity to commercial banking.[47] Yale economist Gary Gorton, for example, refers to firms that lent money in the repo markets as *depositors* and claims that they "were confused about which counterparties were really at risk and consequently ran all banks."[48] Aside from whether it makes sense to refer to the broker-dealers issuing repos as banks in this context, it is absurd to equate retail bank customers who deposit money at federally insured commercial banks with investors in the repo (or commercial paper) market who are investing enormous sums of money in liquid short-term assets precisely so that they can exit the market quickly with as little loss as possible in the event of market turmoil.

It is true, of course, that some of the funds invested through these capital market vehicles end up financing commercial activity and that banks use customer deposits to partially finance commercial activity. In fact, it is also true that equity investments finance commercial activity and that the wages employers pay ultimately help to finance such activity as well (e.g., through bank deposits and MMFs). Nonetheless, it would be strange to equate either equity investments or wages to bank deposits—as shadow banking enthusiasts do with repo financing, for example—simply because they help finance commercial businesses. Thus, the shadow banking metaphor ignores banks' role in capital markets and unnecessarily blurs the distinction between depository institutions (commercial banks) and nonbank intermediaries.[49] The two segments serve distinct financial intermediation roles, are highly regulated in different ways for different reasons, and have been interconnected and reliant on each other for many years.[50]

Naturally, it would be irresponsible simply to assume that the type of regulation in either sector is optimal for that sector or that it would be appropriate for other market segments. In fact, any evaluation of how effectively U.S. financial markets have been regulated must acknowledge that each sector—banking and capital markets—developed as it did partly because of the legal framework that regulated commercial banks more heavily than nonbank financial firms.[51] Partly because of those bank regulations, many people sought a more affordable way to finance their short-term needs outside the banking sector, and numerous investors wanted a higher return than commercial bank savings accounts could offer.

This arrangement meant that more-robust capital market options complemented bank lending. Such increased diversity should have made financial markets more resilient, and federal banking regulators even sanctioned those shadow banking activities. There is good reason, then, to further question the conventional story of the 2008 financial crisis. Given the widespread use of this explanation, it is natural to assume that government reports and academic papers are packed with empirical evidence to support its every aspect. Surprisingly, the opposite is true.

2

ASTOUNDING LACK OF
EVIDENCE FOR CONTAGION

The main justification for many of the financial regulations imposed after 2008 was that panic-fueled instability in one financial sector destabilized other, otherwise healthy market segments, a phenomenon commonly referred to as *contagion*. Multiple government reports, for example, repeat the idea that a rush to redeem shares in one MMF (the Reserve Primary Fund) caused a panicked rush to redeem shares throughout the MMF industry, as well as the idea that instability in the MMF sector caused broader financial market turmoil. Nonetheless, a close examination of the record demonstrates that virtually all of these official reports repeat the same basic MMF contagion story while providing nothing more than assertions.

For instance, a 2020 PWG report states that "there was a run on certain types of MMFs after the failure of Lehman Brothers [in September 2008] caused a large prime MMF [the Reserve Primary Fund] that held Lehman Brothers short-term instruments to sustain losses and 'break the buck'" and that those share redemptions "contributed to dislocations in short-term funding markets."[52] Yet the report provides no evidence to support this MMF contagion story. Instead, the report directs readers to a 2010 PWG report for a "more detailed discussion of the MMF–related events in 2008."[53]

The 2010 report, in turn, makes assertions and fails to provide evidence of MMF contagion in 2008. In fact, it devotes less than 2 full pages (out of 39) to the details of the events during 2008.[54] The report states that "when the Reserve Primary Fund broke the buck in September 2008, it helped ignite a massive run on prime MMFs that contributed to severe dislocations in short–term credit markets and strains on the businesses and institutions that obtain funding in those markets."[55] While the 2010 PWG report does explain—accurately—that billions of dollars flowed out of prime institutional MMFs during the 2008 crisis, it does not provide evidence that the run on the Reserve Primary Fund caused these outflows or that the larger run on MMFs caused problems throughout short–term credit markets and the economy.

Other government reports follow this pattern of making assertions without providing supporting evidence, particularly with respect to MMFs. For instance, the 2012 Financial Stability Oversight Council (FSOC) report states that "the 2007–2008 financial crisis demonstrated that MMFs are susceptible to runs that can have destabilizing implications for financial markets and the economy."[56] The 2012 FSOC report also claims that "the conduct and nature of MMFs' activities and practices make MMFs vulnerable to destabilizing runs, which may spread quickly among funds, impairing liquidity broadly and curtailing the availability of short–term credit."[57] The report then provides a carefully worded footnote that appears to support these claims but still fails to provide the evidence for its MMF contagion story.

The footnote states, "The inherent fragility and susceptibility of MMFs to destabilizing runs has been the subject of considerable academic research and commentary."[58]

It then provides 11 publicly available references. The foot-note is entirely accurate in that such problems with MMFs, especially during the 2008 crisis, have been endlessly inves-tigated. However, a close examination reveals that only five of the references are to empirical papers and that none of the five papers studies whether MMF runs caused problems in other short-term credit markets during 2008 (or other types of MMF contagion effects). Moreover, one of these papers studies the types of risks that MMFs exhibit and reports that runs on MMFs in 2008 were not indiscriminate (for either institutional or retail investors), thus providing evidence against the contagion story.[59] Among the nonem-pirical works cited in the 2012 FSOC report is a comment letter submitted to the SEC by the Squam Lake Group, a group of academics that advocates for stricter MMF regula-tion. Another citation is the prepared remarks for a Senate hearing by one of the members of the Squam Lake Group, and a third item is a speech by Eric Rosengren, past presi-dent of the Federal Reserve Bank of Boston and advocate for stricter MMF regulations.

To their credit, most of the government reports accu-rately describe the large outflows from MMFs during the 2008 crisis. These outflows alone, however, do not provide evidence for MMF contagion; they reveal little about what caused the share redemptions. In fact, several of the reports discuss these outflows and inadvertently provide evidence against the contagion story.[60] For example, the 2012 FSOC report notes:

> Outflows from institutional prime MMFs following the Lehman bankruptcy tended to be larger among MMFs with sponsors that were themselves under stress, indicating that MMF investors redeemed shares when concerned about sponsors' potential inabilities

to bolster ailing funds. These run dynamics were primarily prevalent among the more sophisticated, risk-averse institutional investors, as institutional funds accounted for 95 percent of the net redemptions from prime funds.[61]

The report also claims that "MMFs managed by just a dozen firms accounted for almost three-quarters of the $202 billion decline in the industry's holdings" of commercial paper and that just "five MMF sponsors accounted for almost half of the decline."[62] Together, these facts provide evidence against contagion—virtually all the outflows were among primarily large, sophisticated investors, and those investors did not run indiscriminately, a prerequisite for the contagion story.

Several government reports make an even stronger assertion by saying that these extremely large MMF outflows led to "frozen" short-term credit markets, implying that it was literally impossible to obtain credit. The 2010 PWG report, for example, notes that during September 2008, "MMFs reduced their holdings of commercial paper by about $170 billion (25 percent)" and then claims that (with the exception of overnight lending) "short-term credit markets froze."[63] There is no doubt that short-term credit markets—in both the banking and the nonbanking sectors—experienced a great deal of tumultuous change between 2006 and 2008. Nonetheless, the evidence shows that the PWG report grossly exaggerates those problems by claiming that short-term credit markets froze. In fact, much of the evidence demonstrates that these markets worked precisely as they were designed to function, allowing the most risk-averse investors to seek alternatives that they deemed safer, though often at a cost higher than normal.

Regarding MMFs, a 2016 *American Economic Review* article reports that prime MMF flows differed greatly by size and investor type during September 2008.[64] Using daily data, the paper demonstrates that "massive redemptions" during the weeks surrounding the Lehman Brothers failure "are highly concentrated among a small subset of funds,"[65] with smaller MMFs experiencing greater outflows than larger ones. On September 17, 2008, two days after Lehman filed for bankruptcy, redemptions in MMFs at the 10th percentile (by size) exceeded 15 percent of prior-day total assets, while redemptions in MMFs at the median were approximately 2 percent of prior-day total assets.[66] At the very least, these data suggest that the "run" on MMFs was not a uniform rush to redeem shares in a panic.[67]

Separately, even though it may be difficult to believe given the pervasiveness of the contagion story, many prime MMFs gained assets around the time of the Lehman failure and the Reserve Primary Fund's breaking of the buck. As an SEC report confirms, "the mean prime money market fund experienced large weekly net redemptions, and many individual funds experienced weekly net redemptions that exceeded 10 percent; nevertheless, there were many individual prime funds that experienced weekly net purchases that exceeded 5 and 10 percent of fund assets during the Crisis Month [defined as September 2, 2008, to October 7, 2008]."[68] Put differently, prime MMFs did lose assets overall during this period, but many individual prime MMFs simultaneously gained assets. This finding shows that the markets did not freeze, and it is also inconsistent with a general contagion among MMFs.

Other short-term credit market data similarly demonstrate that these markets did not freeze, even as they came under severe stress. For instance, Federal Reserve data show that total outstanding commercial paper fell by $207 billion through the latter half of September 2008 (with declines of $50.7 billion for the week ending September 17, $61.6 billion the week ending September 24, and $95.0 billion the week ending October 1). While this net reduction represents 11 percent of the total commercial paper outstanding at the beginning of September, $1.6 trillion in commercial paper remained outstanding as of October 1.

It is inaccurate to refer to a $200 billion net reduction as a "frozen" commercial paper market both because of its overall size and because of the short-term nature of commercial paper. For instance, in 2008, 69 percent of outstanding commercial paper had a maturity of 1 to 4 days, and 75 percent had a maturity of less than 9 days.[69] Applying these percentages to even the smallest amount of commercial paper outstanding during either 2008 or 2009 ($1.1 trillion as of July 29, 2009) suggests that approximately $800 billion represented new commercial paper issues. Thus, many firms and investors continued using the commercial paper market throughout the crisis, even as many others exited that market.

Moreover, the same data series shows similar and even larger outflows in commercial paper at other points in time before September 2008. For instance, there was a total net decline of $126 billion from the week ending March 12, 2008, to the week ending May 14, 2008; a net decrease of $98 billion from the week ending November 7, 2007, to the week ending December 19, 2007; and a net decline of $367 billion from the week ending August 15, 2007, to the week ending September 26, 2007. This net decrease of $367 billion in 2007 represents 17 percent of the total commercial paper outstanding at the beginning of August 2007 and is much larger than the September 2008 decrease that followed Lehman's collapse.[70]

In addition to raw data, multiple studies demonstrate that the ABCP market, the hardest hit segment of the commercial paper market, did not freeze. Even a paper authored by Federal Reserve Board researchers that refers to the "collapse" of the ABCP market shows that maturities of new issues declined through the period, meaning that the market did not freeze, and reports that "for the programs that could issue, yield spreads and maturities of new issues had explainable variation during the crisis."[71] The paper also provides evidence that "runs in the crisis were not random but instead were significantly more likely at riskier programs, based on observable program characteristics, program type, sponsor type, and macro-financial variables."[72]

Another study shows that, after the total outstanding ABCP dropped by $1.3 trillion between August and December 2007, the average maturity of ABCP outstanding "declined from 32 days to 15 days over the same period."[73] This finding, of course, shows that firms were still issuing new commercial paper, only with shorter maturities (as would be expected amid market turmoil), meaning that the market did not freeze. The authors also state that their main conclusion, "somewhat surprisingly," is that "the crisis had a profoundly negative effect on commercial banks" and that losses did not transfer to outside investors in ABCP.[74]

Despite so many government officials blaming the crisis on the "shadow banking industry," the authors of the study document that highly regulated commercial banks were a leading originator of commercial paper conduits and that the banks typically provided guarantees to ensure that the commercial paper they issued would receive an investment-grade rating. The same paper explains that the "liquidity guarantees would cover most assets' credit and liquidity risks and effectively absorb all losses of outside investors."[75] Thus, commercial paper investors had protected themselves with bank guarantees, and as the market turmoil increased, they further protected themselves by investing in commercial paper with shorter maturities.

Some of the most frequently cited academic research dealing with the 2008 crisis is that of Gary Gorton, who authored and coauthored many studies, most of which focused on the repo market. Although he is one of the more prolific 2008 financial crisis researchers, Gorton does not demonstrate that contagion caused the 2008 crisis, and his work explicitly absolves MMFs of causing the meltdown. A 2020 paper, for example, reports that MMFs "did not contribute to the drop in net repo funding" and even finds that MMF repo assets increased during the crisis period.[76]

Writing in 2009, Gorton claimed that the "'shadow banking system' at the heart of the current credit crisis is, in fact, a real banking system—and is vulnerable to a banking panic."[77] As for the events that Gorton refers to, the paper is somewhat imprecise. While it acknowledges that a shock caused a panic in 2007 and argues that "the shock to fundamentals was the failure of home prices to rise,"[78] the paper also claims that "the particular design of subprime mortgages made them especially sensitive to house prices" and that "the shock to subprime per se was not the cause of the panic."[79] Ignoring the fact that home prices declined in 2006, the paper states that other asset classes "only experience difficulties when there are problems in the interbank market, starting in August 2007."[80] However, it is unclear whether Gorton uses "interbank market" to refer to the one used by depository institutions (i.e., the federal funds market) or merely to the repo market which, in his view, is part of a "real banking system."

In other research published in 2009, Gorton refers to "the current financial crisis" as a "system-wide bank run" and argues that "the banking sector became insolvent."[81] The paper claims that a run took place in the "securitized banking system" and that it occurred specifically when participants in the repo market decided to stop issuing new debt. While the paper argues that "contagion led to 'withdrawals' in the form of unprecedented high repo haircuts and even the cessation of repo lending on many forms of collateral," it merely claims that the "evidence of insolvency in 2008 is the bankruptcy or forced rescue of several large firms, with other (even larger) firms requiring government support to stay in business."[82]

In separate work that provides further detail on the Lehman failure, Gorton claims that "firms hoarded cash" and cites a Bank for International Settlements (BIS) paper that reports "a contraction of $423 billion in the U.S. dollar interbank borrowing market."[83] The BIS paper does not, however, refer specifically to the repo market; it refers, instead, to the interbank lending market as it is traditionally known, in which depository institutions lend overnight reserve balances to each other.[84] Importantly, Federal Reserve researchers have documented that the U.S. interbank lending market did not freeze and that it did not contract in an indiscriminate manner.[85]

Gorton also likens repo market runs to traditional bank runs. He states that depositors "were firms that lent money in the repo market" and that they "were confused about which counterparties were really at risk and consequently ran all banks."[86] Thus, it does appear that Gorton is referring to the interbank lending market as the repo market. However, he also argues that the "evidence [that depositors were confused] is that non–subprime related asset classes saw their spreads rise significantly only when the interbank market started to break down."[87] Gorton claims that the panic was a systemic event because the whole banking system was insolvent and then rhetorically asks, "How do we know that the banking system was insolvent?"[88] His answer, in full, is that "there is *no direct evidence* [emphasis added], although back–of–the–envelope calculations suggest that the banking system needed to replace about $2 trillion of financing when the repo market haircuts rose."[89]

In the same paper, Gorton's indirect evidence relies on an empirical measure (used in many studies) known as the LIBOR-OIS spread, the difference "between the three-month LIBOR [London Interbank Offered Rate] and the three-month overnight index swap (OIS)."[90] Gorton argues:

> The LIBOR-OIS spread jumps in August 2007, and again when Lehman fails. Other securitized asset classes, with nothing to do with subprime, like credit card receivables, auto loans, and student loans, all move with the proxy for the state of the inter-bank market, not with the ABX. The key question for understanding the panic is: Why were non-subprime-related asset classes affected?[91]

In other words, Gorton's evidence is the empirical finding that the LIBOR-OIS spread jumped in 2007 and again in 2008, when Lehman Brothers filed for bankruptcy, and that the increased spread is correlated with movements in nonsubprime securitized assets, none of which are correlated with movements in a subprime MBS index (the ABX). This indirect evidence is far from convincing, especially given the multiple problems that surfaced in both financial markets (in the banking and nonbanking sectors) and the macroeconomy between 2006 and 2008 and the fact that the repo market is related to short-term financing "for a wide range of securitization activities and financial institutions."[92] Put differently, it is very difficult to discern precisely what information the LIBOR-OIS spread conveys, especially during a crisis.

It is also problematic that the LIBOR-OIS spread corresponds to multiple terms in Gorton's research. On page 10 of a National Bureau of Economic Research paper, for instance, Gorton and a colleague state that the spread "is a proxy for fears about bank solvency,"[93] while on page 11 they refer to the same metric as a "proxy for the state of the interbank market and, in particular, the repo market."[94] Conversely, on page 13 he claims that the LIBOR-OIS spread should be thought of "as a state variable for counterparty risk in the banking system."[95] Perhaps more revealing, though, in 2020, Gorton and coauthors acknowledged, "we do not have anywhere near the data needed to fully understand what happened [in the securitized banking sector during the 2008 crisis]."[96]

Regardless of Gorton's stated caveats, a major problem with relying so heavily on a metric such as the LIBOR-OIS spread is that all interest rate spreads can capture much more than the narrowly defined risk category that such a variable is supposed to represent. Although financial researchers commonly rely on credit spreads to proxy for risk, they have always acknowledged the difficulty in explaining what drives credit spreads. Studies demonstrate, for instance, that the factors "that should in theory determine credit spread changes have rather limited explanatory power."[97] Moreover, LIBOR is a survey-based measure that represents a rate that banks expect they will be offered for unsecured funds, but it is not the rate that they pay. Research also shows that, especially during crises, LIBOR fails to capture the risks that many individual financial firms face—or the costs that banks experience to borrow—on the basis of their own individual characteristics and circumstances.[98]

In fact, the wide range of risk categories that people proxy with interest rate spreads was recently on display during the COVID-19 pandemic. On March 9, 2020, Bloomberg reported that because of "the coronavirus and a plunge in oil prices," the LIBOR-OIS spread had "spiked to its widest level in more than eight years."[99] In December 2020, the PWG report referred to those widening spreads as a sign of increased stress in MMFs and also noted that MMFs experienced "unusually large redemptions" beginning March 12, 2020, after spreads had started increasing.[100] Even if the precise timing of the increased spread is ignored, something such as the LIBOR-OIS spread cannot uniquely identify problems inherent to the MMF sector or the repo market and the general fear over coronavirus and decreasing oil prices.

Other academic researchers have published books on the 2008 crisis, most of which follow the same patterns as the official government reports. That is, they tend to recount massive outflows of funds from short-term credit markets, assert that such outflows are the result of contagion, fail to provide evidence to support such claims, and then emphasize the importance of stemming contagion with expansive government action. One such popular book is *Connectedness and Contagion: Protecting the Financial System from Panics*, by Harvard's Hal Scott. It argues that contagion (infectious runs that indiscriminately propagate throughout the economy, thus harming otherwise healthy markets and solvent firms) was the primary driver of the 2008 crisis and that "the fundamental stability of our financial system" depends on "the ability of the government, and especially our central bank, the Federal Reserve, to deal with panic runs—contagion—as it did during the financial crisis of 2008."[101]

According to Scott, the book "*demonstrates* [emphasis added] that it was 'contagion,' not 'connectedness,' that was the most potentially destructive feature of that crisis and that contagion remains the most virulent and important part of systemic risk still facing the financial system today."[102] In the second chapter of the book, Scott promises to discuss the evidence of the "substantial contagion effects" in the financial system and then provides the following narrative:

> These effects were transmitted initially through the Reserve Primary Fund (RPF) to other prime money market funds; certain segments of the asset-backed, financial, and corporate commercial paper markets; and unsecured interbank lending and secured repo borrowing markets. Ultimately, they resulted in serious runs on other investment banks as investor confidence in the vitality of the independent investment banking business model deteriorated.[103]

Thus, Scott claims that the Reserve Primary Fund, when it "broke the buck," caused a panic (contagion) that spread throughout most short-term capital markets and the banking sector. Given Scott's thesis, it is somewhat surprising that only one chapter—11 pages out of 440—is devoted explicitly to contagion during the 2008 crisis.[104]

It is astonishing, though, that the book provides so little evidence for contagion and ignores the evidence counter to contagion. For instance, the book quotes Jean-Claude Trichet, the president of the European Central Bank, who argues that the lack of specific information during contagion runs can lead to failures of other intermediaries, even those not invested in the same assets or subject to the same original shock.[105] Similarly, it references a speech by Ben Bernanke that retells the conventional story of 2008, complete with severe funding problems in short-term credit markets after the Lehman failure. The book also claims, without providing a reference of any kind, that after the Reserve Primary Fund broke the buck, "contagion effects spread from the money market funds to the ABCP, interbank lending, and secured repo markets as well as to other areas of the non-depository banking system."[106]

Later, in a section on MMF reform, the book states that "there is a legitimate concern, based on our experience in the crisis, that a run on money market funds could spark contagion in the rest of the financial system apart from any connectedness" and that it is therefore "a proper object of policy to minimize the possibility of prime money market fund runs."[107] Yet the book fails to provide empirical evidence that contagion caused any of the declines in short-term credit markets or that the Reserve Primary Fund's breaking of the buck led to (or was caused by) contagion. As do many other works, the book references research papers and official government reports, but most of those simply take for granted that MMF runs sparked contagion (or were caused by it) and that federal involvement successfully ended the panic. For example, Scott references the 2010 PWG report and the 2012 FSOC report, both of which, as described previously, repeat the conventional story about the 2008 crisis without providing any evidence.

One of the only exceptions is that Scott's book references a 2013 working paper to support the hypothesis that prime MMF investors "generated self-fulfilling contagious runs immediately after the Lehman collapse."[108]

That working paper does, in fact, provide evidence that federal backing through the Treasury's Temporary Guarantee Program (TGP) had a positive effect even on MMFs that did not enroll in the TGP, thus helping to identify "the flip side of contagious runs."[109] In 2020, however, the research was published in a peer-reviewed journal, and the published version of the paper demonstrates that "the already-enrolled [in the TGP] funds experienced a relative reduction in fund flows after investors learned their funds had enrolled earlier than other peer funds."[110] Aside from whether the stigma from enrolling in the TGP outweighed any enhancements to stability, this finding demonstrates that investors actually did discriminate against funds (even those in the same family of funds) that they perceived to be riskier. Thus, the research provides evidence against a general contagion effect and even suggests that government intervention can have negative effects that are not immediately recognized during the crisis.

The remainder of the chapter provides only one additional citation for evidence of contagion: the 2012 work of Gorton and his Yale colleague Andrew Metrick that focuses on the repo market. As discussed in a previous section, this work appears to support the contagion hypothesis, but it is carefully caveated and its case is far from strong.[111] In fact, contrary to Gorton and Metrick's work, other evidence weighs in against contagion and suggests that the problems in the repo market did not play a central role in the crisis. This evidence suggests that, instead, the magnitude of the contraction was much greater in the ABCP market, and its severity was much worse because of the close connection between ABCP and (especially the largest) commercial banks.[112] The research demonstrates that only the dealer banks with relatively high shares of agency collateral (versus Treasury securities) maxed out their borrowing capacity from the Fed's Term Securities Lending Facility (TSLF) and Primary Dealer Credit Facility (PDCF), suggesting that dealers faced problems rolling over their short-term debt because of specific types of collateral, not because their counterparties indiscriminately panicked.[113]

These findings are further bolstered by the fact that commercial bank conduits (shell companies managed by commercial banks) were responsible for issuing the majority of ABCP. As of January 2007, for instance, 67 of the 127 sponsors rated by Moody's Investors Service were commercial banks, accounting for 74 percent of outstanding ABCP ($911 billion).[114] Moreover, most of the ABCP issuance was concentrated in the largest institutions—the 10 largest commercial bank sponsors of ABCP accounted for 37 percent of the total ABCP outstanding.[115] Collectively these findings suggest that, even if successful, regulatory policies designed to minimize the probability of runs on prime MMFs—the preferred policy prescription of Scott and many others—would do little to mitigate broader financial crises.

Perhaps inadvertently, Scott's book provides more evidence *against* contagion as a cause of the problems in the commercial paper market. For example, the book states that "the contraction in commercial paper was sustained across all segments of the market, with the *sharpest declines* [emphasis added] seen in asset-backed and financial commercial paper outstanding."[116] Indeed, the decline was much sharper in ABCP than in other commercial paper segments, suggesting that both buyers and sellers of commercial paper became particularly wary of one segment of the market.

Put differently, this sharp differential in the decline across types of commercial paper suggests that market participants did not indiscriminately panic, as they would during a bout of contagion.

Similarly, the fact that the corporate commercial paper market suffered much less disruption (as Scott mentions) also works against the broad contagion hypothesis, as does the fact (also referenced by Scott) that nonfinancial firms were still able to rely on bank lending. Despite these facts, Scott insists that "the impact on money market funds and the partial paralysis of commercial paper markets in the aftermath of the RPF debacle thus began to spill directly into the nonfinancial economy as contagion effects were transmitted to capital markets for corporate borrowing."[117] Scott provides no evidence for this proposition other than to cite a bankruptcy attorney's statement before the Financial Crisis Inquiry Commission. Similarly, he identifies the "post-Lehman contagion" as the problem that "afflicted short-term interbank lending and the repo market" but again fails to cite any empirical evidence to support the thesis.[118] Another problem with this post-Lehman contagion story is that, according to the SEC, investors had already started rushing to redeem shares in prime MMFs on September 12, days *before* the Lehman failure.[119]

There is no doubt that Scott's book thoroughly discusses the large declines in borrowing and the interest rate swings that occurred during the 2008 crisis. Still, the fact that borrowing declined—or that LIBOR rates, the LIBOR-OIS spread, and the TED spread (each a proxy for interbank lending risk) all increased—does not demonstrate that contagion caused the turmoil in these credit markets. Likewise, the mere fact that many banks pulled back from interbank lending markets does not show that contagion caused them to do so, and the evidence from the U.S. interbank lending market, which Scott's book does not mention, shows that banks did, in fact, exit that market on the basis of individual (counterparty) bank characteristics.[120]

Although the economics literature has produced essentially no empirical evidence that contagion in any part of the short-term credit markets caused the 2008 financial crisis, it is abundantly clear that problems in the asset-backed credit markets were at the heart of the turmoil. While the contagion story tends to ignore the problematic signs that occurred before either the Lehman failure or the run on the Reserve Primary Fund, those signs were plentiful.

3

ALTERNATIVES TO THE CONTAGION STORY

It is impossible to prove that contagion can never occur, but the evidence suggests that problems in specific asset markets, rather than general contagion, caused the broader short-term credit problems that became the 2008 financial crisis. Similarly, the evidence suggests that discriminant runs on MMFs—not panicked share redemptions—occurred after the Lehman failure. Naturally, this alternative description leaves unanswered the question of what caused those specific problems. Unfortunately, so many negative events took place prior to Lehman Brothers' 2008 bankruptcy that it is difficult to blame the run on prime MMFs on any single event. It is even harder, for that matter, to blame the broader credit market problems during the crisis on any single event.

Some troubling economic news surfaced nearly two years prior to September 2008. The conventional story of the 2008 crisis essentially ignores these events and subjectively attributes credit market difficulties to a handful of events in 2008, such as Lehman's failure or the run on the Reserve Primary Fund. But by late 2007, it was obvious that market participants were viewing the economic and financial problems as anything but minor. The following list provides an overview of the most well-known of these problematic events, including several that occurred in the traditional banking sector.

Ownit Mortgage Solutions

In December 2006, Ownit Mortgage Solutions, the 11th largest subprime lender in the United States, filed for bankruptcy and laid off its 700 workers.[121] News reports revealed that "Merrill Lynch & Co., JPMorgan Chase & Co., Credit Suisse First Boston and other mortgage purchasers were demanding that Ownit buy back more than $165 million in loans on which borrowers had missed payments" and stated that "Ownit's demise is an example of wider troubles among independent subprime lenders, which, unlike more diversified banking companies, depend heavily on Wall Street for loans and services."[122] The *Los Angeles Times* reported that "several other national subprime firms have closed, among them Mortgage Lenders Network USA Inc., a Middletown, Conn.-based lender that shut down Tuesday" and that "numerous subprime companies are reportedly on the auction block, including Irvine-based Option One Mortgage, a unit of H&R Block Inc., and ACC Capital Corp., the private holding company for Ameriquest Mortgage Co. and affiliates."[123]

New Century Financial

In April 2007, New Century Financial filed bankruptcy "amid a surge in homeowner defaults," and the California-based company fired more than 3,000 employees (over half of its workforce).[124] Reuters reported that "New Century was the largest independent U.S. provider of 'subprime' mortgages, or home loans to people with poor credit histories" and that "more than 30 rivals have sold or closed similar operations in the past year."[125] The story quoted a market analyst who warned that "we are only at the very beginning of the problems facing subprime. This liquidity crisis is continuing."[126]

Bear Stearns, Part 1

In June 2007, the *New York Times* reported that Bear Stearns had pledged more than $3 billion "to bail out one of its hedge funds that was collapsing because of bad bets on subprime mortgages."[127] The pledge represented the largest such effort since the 1998 Long-Term Capital Management rescue.[128] The story demonstrated that these problems surfaced prior to June, noting that "the most startling development was a sharp restatement in April of the second [larger] fund," when Bear "revalued some securities and told investors that the fund was down 23 percent, not 10 percent as it had said earlier."[129] Investors immediately began demanding to pull out their money, and in May, Bear froze all redemption requests.

Countrywide Financial/Bank of America

In January 2008, at least four months after Countrywide had publicly acknowledged major financial difficulties, Bank of America purchased the company so that Countrywide could avoid filing bankruptcy. In August 2007, Countrywide had to use its "entire $11.5 billion credit line from a consortium of banks because it could no longer sell or borrow against home loans it has made," and "Bank of America invested $2 billion for a 16 percent stake in Countrywide."[130] Shortly after, the company "was forced to choose between bankruptcy or being acquired by Bank of America."[131] The *New Yorker* also reported that "as 2007 progressed, subprime defaults escalated rapidly, and Wall Street bankers abandoned the mortgage-backed securities they had prized, and their supplier, too," cutting off Countrywide's short-term funding.[132]

Washington Mutual

In the fourth quarter of 2007, Seattle-based savings and loan bank Washington Mutual wrote down $1.6 billion in defaulted mortgages, resulting in a $1.9 billion net loss for the fourth quarter.[133] Even though the bank was Federal Deposit Insurance Corporation (FDIC) insured, Washington Mutual also experienced a run by its retail bank customers who, over a 10-day period, "withdrew $16.7 billion [more than 11 percent of the bank's total deposits] out of their savings and checking accounts."[134]

BNP Paribas (and Other European Problems)

On August 9, 2007, Reuters reported that "France's biggest listed bank, BNP Paribas, froze [prevented investors from redeeming] 1.6 billion euros ($2.2 billion) worth of funds on Thursday, citing the U.S. subprime mortgage sector woes that have rattled financial markets worldwide."[135] The report also stated that "later in the day a separate European fund valued at 750 million euros was frozen too, and a Dutch bank pulled its planned new listing after suffering subprime losses. This latest subprime fallout came as Germany's Bundesbank held a meeting of those involved in the rescue of Europe's highest profile subprime victim yet, lender IKB, and as the European Central Bank said it stood ready to act if needed to ensure smooth functioning of markets."[136]

Northern Rock

On September 13, 2007, retail customers of United Kingdom–based bank Northern Rock lined up to remove their deposits, and on the following day, the Bank of England announced it would provide emergency liquidity support for Northern Rock. Managers had informed British banking regulators of funding problems at least as early as August 13, 2007, and the bank was relying on the same types of conduits that many U.S. commercial banks were using to finance their operations.[137]

American Home Mortgage

According to the *New York Times*, "At the start of the year [2007], American Home Mortgage seemed to defy the problems that were plaguing its industry. In the first three months, the company made $16.7 billion in home loans, up 27.2 percent from the same period in 2006."[138] In August 2007, American Home Mortgage closed, and the *Times* reported that the company would lay off all but 750 of its 7,000 employees "in light of liquidity issues resulting from disruptions in the secondary mortgage market."[139]

Accredited Home Lenders

In August 2007, Accredited Home Lenders Holding, "a San Diego-based subprime mortgage company being acquired by Lone Star Funds, said that its own sale was in jeopardy and that bankruptcy was possible."[140] The company announced, "Several of our competitors have recently stopped originating loans or sought protection under bankruptcy laws," and "we may suffer a similar fate."[141]

Merrill Lynch

In the third quarter of 2007, long before it was forced to merge with Bank of America, Merrill Lynch reported major asset write-downs. As reported in *Forbes*, "By the time the third quarter of 2007 rolled around the firm came to the grave realization that, not only was the value of these securities less than what was being presented to shareholders and regulators on its balance sheet, but, in fact, the firm had no clear idea what (if anything) these bonds might actually be worth."[142] Merrill reported almost $8.5 billion in securities write-offs, "resulting in a $7.9 billion loss for the quarter."[143] Then, in the fourth quarter of 2007, "Merrill would go on to lose an additional $8.6 billion," and the company ended the year "more than $10 billion in the red."[144]

Citigroup

On December 13, 2007, Reuters reported that Citigroup planned to take $49 billion in mortgage-security-related structured investment vehicles (SIVs) back onto its balance sheet, "a move that further strains the biggest U.S. banking group's capital levels and may scupper a U.S. government-endorsed SIV bailout plan."[145] Reuters also reported that "fears about Citi's assets have contributed to

the 44 percent decline in Citi's shares this year, about double the decline of the broader banking sector," and that
"Moody's estimated earlier this month that the SIV sector's
assets globally had fallen to just under $300 billion from
$370 billion in July."[146]

Ambac

In January 2008, one of the largest U.S. bond insurers,
Ambac, reported a $3.3 billion loss. According to Reuters,
"Ambac Financial Group Inc reported a quarterly loss of
$3.3 billion on Tuesday after recording massive credit deriv-
ative write-downs," and the company "said it hopes to find
much-needed capital 'reasonably soon.'"[147] The report also
stated that "Ambac's trouble came after it used credit derivatives to guarantee a series of portfolios of asset-backed securities" and that many of those securities "were linked to
subprime mortgages" that "have weakened dramatically in
the widening credit crisis."[148]

Bear Stearns, Part 2

On March 16, 2008, the Fed provided a loan to Bear Stearns
through JPMorgan Chase. The funds effectively guaranteed
$30 billion in MBSs so that JPMorgan would buy the firm
and, thus, Bear Stearns could avoid a bankruptcy filing.[149]
Fed Chairman Ben Bernanke also announced that the Fed
took this action to help prevent a broader financial crisis,
noting that "the sudden failure of Bear Stearns likely would
have led to a chaotic unwinding of positions in those markets and could have severely shaken confidence," with negative effects being "felt broadly in the real economy."[150]

IndyMac

In what was at the time the largest bank failure in U.S. history, the FDIC closed IndyMac Bancorp on July 11, 2008. Even though the bank's deposits were FDIC insured, retail customers ran on the bank to pull their money out. As the *New York Times* reported, IndyMac was "the first major bank to shut its doors since the mortgage crisis erupted more than a year ago."[151] The California-based bank laid off more than half of its 7,200 employees.[152]

Fannie Mae and Freddie Mac

The Federal Housing Finance Agency placed Fannie Mae and Freddie Mac, by far the dominant credit purveyors in the U.S. secondary mortgage market, in government conservatorship on September 6, 2008.[153]

AIG

The federal government provided a bailout for American International Group (AIG) on September 16, 2008, but problems had occurred at the insurer—problems involving the company's ability to continue financing its operations—long before the government intervened. As the *New York Times* reported, "The Securities and Exchange Commission is examining the payment demands that a number of firms—most prominently Goldman—made during 2007 and 2008 as the mortgage market imploded."[154] In the official statement regarding its intervention, the Federal Reserve referred to the fact that "short-term funding markets had come under severe stress" in the "months prior to September 2008" and that the stress had placed "significant liquidity pressures on AIG that hindered its ability to obtain adequate funding from *banking institutions* [emphasis added] or in the market, and threatened to prompt a default by the firm."[155]

Lehman Brothers and Reserve Primary Fund

On September 15, 2008, the Fed decided against helping Lehman Brothers, allowing the firm to file for bankruptcy without providing any assistance even though it had assisted Bear Stearns, a much smaller investment bank ($18 billion versus $600 billion). This change in policy unsettled markets, especially given the public knowledge that the federal government was involved in trying to rescue Lehman and that the Fed had already set a clear precedent against allowing large financial firms to fail.[156] In fact, even the SEC had taken actions that suggested that federal regulators would not let Lehman fail, and the press release indicated that the troubled ABSs were not grossly overvalued. On July 15, 2008, the SEC had restricted short sales for the stocks of 19 financial firms, including Lehman. The agency's order began with the warning that "*false* rumors can lead to a loss of confidence in our markets" and later stated that "*false* rumors have continued to threaten significant market disruption" (emphasis added).[157] Nonetheless, when both Barclays and Bank of America were unable to secure federal protection against possible losses (such as those provided to JPMorgan for acquiring Bear Stearns), they withdrew their bids.[158] Lehman filed for bankruptcy the next day— September 15, 2008.[159] It would have been inconsistent, but at least coherent, if the decision to let Lehman fail indicated that the federal government was not going to rescue any additional financial institutions. Instead, the next day, the Federal Reserve announced it would lend (through the New York Fed) up to $85 billion to AIG. On the same day— September 16, 2008—the Reserve Primary Fund broke the buck. Although it is rarely acknowledged, it is a fact that investors had started rushing to redeem shares in prime MMFs on September 12, prior to the Lehman failure.[160]

This list not only shows that several major problems occurred in 2008 prior to Lehman Brothers' failure, but also demonstrates that major credit market problems were pervasive and widely known before the end of 2007. With the large declines in outstanding commercial paper during 2007, it is no surprise that pre-2008 macroeconomic data also reflect these problems. For instance, after growing at more than 2 percent in the first quarter of 2006, gross domestic product (GDP) growth slowed to 1.13 percent in the second quarter of 2006 and then to just 0.85 percent in the third quarter. Growth was essentially flat through the third quarter of 2007 and then slowed for three consecutive quarters, ending with a decrease (negative 0.06 percent) of GDP in the first quarter of 2008. This decline was the first time GDP growth had fallen below zero since the third quarter of 2001.[161]

In the beginning of 2007, the U.S. unemployment rate had essentially started a new, increasing trend. At the end of the fourth quarter in 2006, the unemployment rate was 4.4 percent; at the end of the first quarter in 2007, it was up to 4.5 percent. It remained at 4.5 percent for the second quarter of 2007, increased to 4.7 percent in the third quarter of 2007, and then increased to 4.8 percent in the fourth quarter of 2007. The rate continued to increase, of course, through the fourth quarter of 2009, when it reached

9.9 percent.[162] Similarly, in April 2007, the U.S. employment level declined by 734,000 people, the first major drop since July 2003 and the largest drop since August 2001 (830,000). The level fluctuated, with moderate increases and decreases for several months, until it started a major downward trend in May 2008, with a drop of 224,000. After May 2008, the level declined for 17 consecutive months, until it increased by 227,000 in November 2009.[163]

Perhaps most relevant to the 2008 crisis, U.S. home prices started falling in the summer of 2006. Specifically, growth in the Case-Shiller U.S. National Home Price Index slowed in June and July 2006 (though it was still positive) and then fell in August 2006 by 0.11 percent. The index then declined every month until April 2009.[164] By the first quarter of 2007, defaults on subprime mortgages had risen to a four-year high.[165] Given that overvalued ABSs tied to real estate—many of them closely connected to commercial banks—were at the core of the financial market stress appearing throughout this period, it is difficult to argue that home price declines were not a central cause of the 2008 financial crisis.

Unsurprisingly, several empirical studies do argue that the proximate cause of the crisis was a shock to home prices, and some have tied the decline in employment to a sharp reduction in households' housing net worth. For instance, in a 2014 paper, Atif Mian of Princeton and Amir Sufi of the University of Chicago argue that "deterioration in household balance sheets, or the housing net worth channel, played a significant role in the sharp decline in U.S. employment between 2007 and 2009."[166] The authors also present evidence that, as early as 2007, an increasing number of business owners reported that a lack of sales was their biggest concern, reinforcing that households were no longer spending as much.[167]

Given all these events, it makes little sense to suggest that, for example, the Reserve Primary Fund's breaking of the buck, rather than any combination of the widespread financial market and economic turmoil, caused the problems that occurred after early September 2008. The Reserve Primary Fund shareholders, like all MMF investors, had a surplus of economic and financial problems, as well as inconsistent government intervention policies, providing incentives to invest in the safest possible short-term assets. In fact, the conventional story of the 2008 crisis looks even less realistic after those federal interventions are closely examined. It turns out that the supposed success of those interventions ignores, among other things, the piecemeal fashion in which the federal government escalated its efforts.

4

GOVERNMENT BACKING
NOT A CURE-ALL

The conventional story of the 2008 financial crisis is that after the Reserve Primary Fund broke the buck, contagion quickly spread to other prime MMFs and then to other short-term credit market segments. The panic was arrested, the story goes, only after the federal government provided widespread financial guarantees. On the basis of this account, some scholars and policymakers advocate federal backing for all short-term credit markets, and others even suggest prohibiting investment options such as prime MMFs.[168] Aside from any possible costs or benefits from such federal policies, it is not clear, from what happened during the 2008 crisis, that increased federal backing would work as proponents hope.

It is true, of course, that the federal government took many different actions to support credit markets during this period, ranging from press releases and legislative action to broad programs at the Federal Reserve and outright financial guarantees. For its part, the Federal Reserve provided loans through many broad-based programs and allocated credit directly to several firms. For instance, the Fed provided a $13 billion loan to Bear Stearns, one of the Fed's largest primary dealers, on March 14, 2008. The loan was repaid in days, but then the Fed provided a $30 billion loan to facilitate JPMorgan Chase's acquisition of Bear Stearns (through a special-purpose vehicle named Maiden Lane LLC). Later in the crisis, the government provided several rounds of support to insurance giant AIG. On September 16, 2008, the Fed gave AIG an $85 billion revolving credit line. Then, in October, the Fed created a securities borrowing facility to provide up to $37.8 billion to support "a securities lending program operated by AIG's domestic insurance companies."[169] In November 2008, the U.S. Treasury purchased $40 billion in preferred shares of AIG, and the Fed created two special-purpose vehicles, one that replaced the securities borrowing facility and another that purchased securitized assets from AIG's counterparties. At the very least, the Fed's initial efforts to support AIG were insufficient to allay the concerns of AIG's counterparties.

Separately, the Fed created more than a dozen special lending programs, in many cases by invoking its emergency authority under Section 13(3) of the Federal Reserve Act. The U.S. Government Accountability Office (GAO) estimates that from December 1, 2007, through July 21, 2010, the Fed lent financial firms more than $16 trillion through its broad-based emergency programs.[170] To put this figure in perspective, annual GDP reached $16.8 trillion in 2013, a record high at that time for nominal GDP in the United States. The following list summarizes the major programs that the Federal Reserve created during the 2008 financial crisis and discusses most of the instances in which the Fed provided extraordinary liquidity prior to September 2008, the month that Lehman Brothers failed and the Reserve Primary Fund broke the buck.[171]

Term Auction Facility, December 12, 2007

The Term Auction Facility (TAF) was created to auction one- and three-month discount window loans to depository institutions. The idea was to provide loans at a market-determined rate (instead of at the administered discount rate), thus avoiding the stigma normally attached to borrowing at the Fed's discount window. The Fed provided $40 billion of loans during December 2007 and $995 billion between January 17 and August 28, 2008. Almost $4 trillion was provided through the TAF between 2007 and 2010, but more than $1 trillion of that total was provided prior to Lehman's bankruptcy.[172]

Dollar Swap Lines, December 6, 2007

Even though they do not have large U.S. dollar deposits, many foreign-domiciled commercial banks borrow U.S. dollars to fund purchases of various U.S. dollar-denominated assets. In December 2007, as global credit markets were increasingly disrupted, the European Central Bank and the Swiss National Bank requested dollar swap lines with the Fed so that they could more easily provide U.S. dollar loans to the banks that they served. Under those arrangements, the New York Fed exchanged U.S. dollars for the foreign central bank's currency, and the foreign central bank consented to repurchase its currency at the same exchange rate on an agreed-upon future date. The Fed approved swap lines with 12 other foreign central banks during 2008, and in October, the Fed uncapped the amounts available in the swap lines with "the European Central Bank, the Bank of England, the Swiss National Bank, and the Bank of Japan."[173] The amount outstanding peaked at $580 billion in December 2008, and the Fed closed all 14 lines in February 2010.[174]

In May 2010, the Fed reopened swap lines with five foreign central banks, all of which were supposed to close in January 2011. The end date was extended twice, ultimately leaving the facility available through August 2012.

Term Securities Lending Facility, March 11, 2008

In March 2008, the Fed created the Term Securities Lending Facility (TSLF), designed as "a weekly loan facility that promoted liquidity in Treasury and other collateral markets and thus fostered the functioning of financial markets more generally."[175] Under the terms of the TSLF, the Fed loaned its own Treasury securities—those held by the System Open Market Account (SOMA)—to its primary dealers over a one-month term against other program-eligible general collateral, including agency securities and agency mortgage-backed securities, as well as investment-grade corporate securities, investment-grade municipal securities, investment-grade mortgage-backed securities, and investment-grade ABSs.[176] Between March and August 28, 2008, the Fed lent $712.3 billion in Treasury securities to its primary dealers. By the time the Fed closed the TSLF on February 1, 2010, it had loaned an additional $1.3 trillion.[177]

Primary Dealer Credit Facility, March 17, 2008

In response to problems in the tri-party repo market, the Fed created the Primary Dealer Credit Facility (PDCF) to provide overnight cash loans to primary dealers against eligible collateral. Between March and July 24, 2008, the Fed loaned $1.35 trillion through the PDCF, with Bear Stearns borrowing 71 percent of the total.[178] Nearly $9 trillion was loaned through the PDCF by 2010. Of more than 20 primary dealers, almost 80 percent of all the lending through the PDCF went to just 4 firms: Citigroup Global Markets, Merrill Lynch Government Securities, Morgan Stanley & Co., and Bear Stearns.[179] After the Lehman Brothers failure in September, the Fed broadened the type of collateral accepted for these loans, including equities and speculative-grade debt as collateral in addition to the originally eligible types, such as high-grade bonds and government-sponsored enterprises (GSE)–backed securities.[180]

Asset-Backed Commercial Paper Money Market Mutual Fund Liquidity Facility, September 19, 2008

The Fed used the ABCP MMF Liquidity Facility (AMLF) to support the banking and MMF sectors by providing non-recourse loans (i.e., in the event of a default, the Fed's only remedy was to keep the collateral) that could be used to purchase ABCP from MMFs. In other words, the AMLF was used to make loans to banks so that they could provide liquidity to MMFs. The loans were made available to all U.S. depository institutions, as well as to all U.S. bank holding companies and their broker-dealer affiliates. Between September 19 and October 6, 2008, the Fed lent $165.8 billion through the AMLF. By the time the Fed closed the AMLF on February 1, 2010 (with the last reported loan on May 9, 2008), borrowers had used the facility for a total of $217.3 billion.[181]

Commercial Paper Funding Facility, October 7, 2008

According to the Federal Reserve, "in the fall of 2008, the commercial paper market was under considerable strain as

MMFs and other investors—themselves often facing liquidity pressures—became increasingly reluctant to purchase commercial paper."[182] The Commercial Paper Funding Facility (CPFF) was established to provide liquidity to the commercial paper market by directly purchasing new issues of ABCP from the issuers. By the time the Fed closed the facility on February 1, 2010, it had purchased $738 billion of commercial paper, with most of that amount split somewhat evenly between 2008 ($332 billion) and 2009 ($403 billion).[183]

Term Asset-Backed Securities Loan Facility, November 25, 2008

The Fed designed the Term ABS Loan Facility (TALF) to provide nonrecourse loans to investors so that they could purchase ABSs, with the explicit "intent of reopening the new-issue ABS market."[184] Under the terms of the TALF program, any U.S.-based firm was eligible to borrow, but those funds could be used only to invest in ABSs. According to the Federal Reserve, a "wide range of investors participated, including mutual funds, pension funds, insurance companies, investment funds and hedge funds, and others."[185] The first loans were issued in March 2009, the Fed lent a total of $71 billion through the facility, and there was never "more than $49 billion outstanding at any one time."[186]

While this list demonstrates that the Fed escalated its efforts throughout the crisis, it does not include many other federal interventions, some of which were also undertaken by the Federal Reserve, that occurred during the same months. For instance, although quantitative easing (QE) does not fit neatly into either an individual or a broad-based lending arrangement, the Fed initiated the first of several rounds of QE in December 2008. Aside from whether QE worked as intended, it is impossible to ignore the direct support that QE provided to securitization markets. The first round of QE, for instance, promised to purchase up to $500 billion of Fannie Mae and Freddie Mac MBSs from both GSEs and other financial institutions. In September 2012, the Fed announced a third round of QE, this time making an uncapped commitment to purchase $85 billion per month in (combined) long-term Treasuries, Fannie and Freddie debt, and MBSs.[187]

Distinct from the Federal Reserve's actions, the federal government initiated multiple programs to support individual investors, consumers, and credit markets more broadly. For instance, on September 29, 2008, the U.S. Treasury announced its TGP for MMFs. Under this program, the federal government agreed to guarantee the principal of any eligible MMF (retail or institutional) "that applies for and pays a fee to participate in the program."[188] Separately, as part of the Troubled Asset Relief Program (TARP) enacted on October 3, 2008, Congress temporarily increased the FDIC deposit insurance limit from $100,000 to $250,000, with the higher limit set to revert to $100,000 on December 31, 2010.[189]

Then, on October 14, 2008,[190] outside its normal role as the federal insurer of bank deposits, the FDIC announced the Temporary Liquidity Guarantee Program (TLGP), an initiative that consisted of two components: the Transaction Account Guarantee Program (TAGP) and the Debt Guarantee Program (DGP).[191] The TAGP guaranteed all domestic non–interest-bearing transaction deposits, low-interest negotiable order of withdrawal (NOW) accounts, and Interest on

Lawyers' Trust Accounts (IOLTAs). Originally, the guarantee applied to all such accounts held at participating banks and thrifts through December 31, 2009, but the deadline was later extended and ultimately expired on December 31, 2010. In combination with the FDIC's main deposit insurance program, the TAGP allowed the federal government to temporarily guarantee nearly all bank deposits. However, the typical transaction account balance was approximately $4,000 in 2008, and less than 10 percent of U.S. households held certificates of deposit, with a median balance of just $16,000.[192] It is difficult, therefore, to argue that the TAGP was designed to help typical Americans feel more secure about their bank balances.

Conversely, the DGP provided a federal guarantee for certain types of new debt issued by private firms. Specifically, such a guarantee applied to senior unsecured debt issued between October 14, 2008, and October 31, 2009. The FDIC guarantee for this debt extended through maturity *or* December 31, 2012, whichever came first. Many large financial firms—such as Citigroup, Bank of America, and Goldman Sachs—used the DGP to issue government-guaranteed debt. Throughout the DGP's entire existence, firms issued $345.8 billion of federally guaranteed debt, paying fees of $10.4 billion to the FDIC.

Aside from all the previously mentioned federal involvement, the Federal Home Loan Bank (FHLB) system, another GSE, provided an enormous amount of liquidity (loans referred to as advances) to commercial banks. As Hal Scott's book reports, between "the third and fourth quarters of 2007, FHLB advances outstanding grew by $235 billion, a 36.7 percent increase," and these advances "continued to grow through most of 2008, peaking at over $1 trillion by the end of the third quarter of 2008."[193]

As this history of federal support initiatives demonstrates, many efforts to calm short-term credit markets occurred long before Lehman Brothers filed for bankruptcy and the Reserve Primary Fund broke the buck. Just the FHLB advances and three Federal Reserve facilities (the TAF, the TSLF, and the PDCF) provided $4 trillion in credit prior to Lehman's failure. Yet despite this much government-backed credit (more than 25 percent of 2008 GDP), the amount and scope of federal efforts continued to escalate after September 2008.

Throughout the entire crisis period, the Fed expanded or replaced its facilities designed to help specific markets. It is true that the Fed did not target each of these programs in exactly the same manner, but all of these efforts provided government support to short-term credit markets, frequently by supporting the ABS market, even if indirectly. The constant expansion alone, therefore, is reason enough to question whether all of the federal intervention worked as its designers had intended.

There was good reason to doubt whether federal guarantees for credit markets would work as proponents hoped. For instance, in November 2008, the U.S. Treasury stepped in as a buyer of last resort to help the Reserve Fund's U.S. Government MMF—a fund that was invested only in U.S. government securities and agency debt—sell its securities.[194] This action, of course, came after Treasury had announced its TGP for MMFs, after the Fed had established at least six distinct lending facilities, after the federal government had guaranteed essentially all bank deposits, after the FDIC had issued guarantees on newly issued corporate debt, and after Congress had passed TARP. If government backing is all that is needed to comfort investors, it is unclear why any

MMF would have trouble selling its government securities, even before all these federal efforts.[195]

Indeed, if government backing is all that is needed to quell fears in the market, it is unclear why any government MMF would have difficulty selling its agency MBS, especially after Fannie and Freddie were under federal control. Likewise, it is difficult to explain why, if government backing is sufficient to calm a financial panic, two FDIC banks—Washington Mutual and IndyMac—experienced runs by retail deposit customers during this period despite FDIC backing.[196] At the very least, the evidence suggests that mere provision of federal support—including guarantees—to short-term credit markets is not sufficient to ensure financial stability. Aside from whether federal financial guarantees might work as their proponents intend, the historical record demonstrates that federal intervention heavily contributed to the 2008 crisis.

5

WHAT GAVE RISE TO SO MANY ABSs?

There is no doubt that declining values for ABSs were at the heart of the 2008 financial crisis. In addition to problems with MMFs, the commercial paper market, the repo market, or even the banking sector, overvalued ABSs routinely surface as a main culprit. And, in fact, there was a surge in the use of all kinds of ABSs several years prior to the crisis across short-term credit markets. In the commercial paper market, for example, Federal Reserve data show a distinct increase in the amount of ABCP outstanding starting in 2005.[197] Between January 2005 and July 2007, the total amount of outstanding commercial paper increased by $799 billion, with ABCP accounting for 66 percent of that increase ($525 billion).[198] Thus, it is perfectly natural to ask why this surge in ABS issuance took place.

The conventional story of the 2008 crisis, of course, attributes the jump in ABSs to the supposedly unregulated actions of the shadow banking system.[199] As discussed in a previous section, however, most of this activity took place under the watchful eyes of federal authorities, with the explicit blessing of federal banking regulators. Several distinct regulatory and statutory changes help explain the shift toward the increased use of ABSs, a fact that has not gone entirely unnoticed.

For example, Gorton and Metrick point out in the *Journal of Financial Economics* that, after a federal push to increase subprime mortgages, "in the years 2001–2006, a total of about $2.5 trillion of subprime mortgages were originated" and nearly "half of this total came in 2005 and 2006."[200] Gorton and Metrick also acknowledge that the bankruptcy code gives special status to derivatives (including repo contracts) and that "this bankruptcy safe-harbor was a primary driver of the growth of repo."[201] Likewise, in another article, they point out that the U.S. bankruptcy code was amended in 1984 to allow repo counterparties to liquidate collateral without going through bankruptcy, a feature that gives these counterparties preferential treatment compared to other creditors.[202] Still, the problem is much bigger because the 1984 provision applied only to repo transactions based on Treasuries, agency securities, bank certificates of deposit, and bankers' acceptances.

After enacting the current bankruptcy code in 1978, Congress steadily expanded safe harbors for derivatives and repos, as well as other financial contracts.[203] While the bankruptcy code provides several key protections, such as the *automatic stay* and a prohibition against *preferential transfers*, to help ensure that similarly situated creditors share any losses in an equitable manner, it also provides derivatives and repos with special safe harbors that exclude their counterparties from these protections. In fact, the 2005 Bankruptcy Abuse Prevention and Consumer Protection Act expanded several of these safe harbors by defining the term *swap agreement* to include (effectively) all derivatives contracts. Not only did this change extend safe harbors to virtually all derivatives users such that the entire market was exempt from the automatic stay and key preference provisions, but the 2005 act also expanded the definition of *repurchase agreement* to explicitly include "mortgage related securities . . . mortgage loans, interests in mortgage related securities or mortgage loans."[204]

These safe harbors mean that, beginning in 2005, all derivatives and repo users were protected parties relative to ordinary creditors. The fact that the debtor's counterparties could seize collateral free from these preference protections proved especially harmful during the 2008 crisis. Even though industry advocates originally argued that these safe harbors were necessary to prevent runlike behavior, the 2008 crisis demonstrated that the opposite was true; they encouraged counterparties to run.

Bear Stearns's counterparties, for instance, ran before Bear could even consider bankruptcy, safe in the knowledge that doing so would protect them more than going through bankruptcy proceedings. Similarly, JPMorgan seized $17 billion in Lehman Brothers' collateral (securities and cash), leaving Lehman with no choice but to come up with additional collateral, thus worsening its liquidity position. Lehman could not file bankruptcy to prevent Morgan from selling the collateral because of the safe harbors, and Lehman had no reason to expect that it could retrieve the payment as a special preference if it did file for bankruptcy.[205] The safe harbors also played a negative role in the near failure of AIG when counterparties increasingly demanded additional collateral for their large credit default swap (CDS) portfolio. As with Lehman, AIG would have been able to refuse the collateral demands and expect legal protection had there been no safe harbors for the CDSs.[206]

Other data support the idea that these safe harbors induced firms to rely more heavily on repos after 2005. For instance,

Bear Stearns's liabilities consisted of only 7 percent repos in 1990, but by 2008, they consisted of 25 percent repos.[207] More broadly, the portion of total investment bank assets financed by repos doubled between 2000 and 2007.[208] Ultimately, it's irrelevant whether the growing market led to legislative action to further support the market or whether the legislative amendments to the bankruptcy code led to the growing market. Either way, the market likely would not have supported such high increases in leverage without the special protections afforded in 2005. At the very least, these new ABSs—including ABCP and repos using ABSs for collateral—would have been structured differently had the bankruptcy code not provided special protections.

In addition to these legislative changes to the bankruptcy code, federal banking regulators finalized a rule in 2004 that promoted the issuance of ABCP by commercial banks. A Financial Accounting Standards Board (FASB) review of off–balance sheet items in the wake of the Enron accounting scandal was the driving force behind this regulatory change. In 2003, after nearly two years of review, FASB concluded that if a publicly traded company took an actual risk, that risk should be consolidated and included on the balance sheet. FASB did provide certain exemptions that banks could use, however, so the new standards did not force banks to immediately take all their off–balance sheet items back onto their balance sheets. Still, just to be safe, federal banking regulators gave banks a reason to breathe easy about the future possibility of doing so.

The final rule, issued jointly by the Federal Reserve, the FDIC, the Office of the Comptroller of the Currency (OCC), and the (now-defunct) Office of Thrift Supervision, permitted "sponsoring banks, bank holding companies, and thrifts (banking organizations) to continue to exclude from their risk-weighted asset base for purposes of calculating the risk-based capital ratios asset-backed commercial paper (ABCP) program assets that are consolidated onto sponsoring banking organizations' balance sheets."[209] In other words, federal bank regulators allowed banks favorable capital treatment even if they did have to bring off–balance sheet ABCP assets back onto their balance sheets because of the new FASB decision. The final rule made federal banking regulators' position very clear:

> The agencies believe that the consolidation of ABCP program assets generally would result in risk-based capital requirements that do not appropriately reflect the risks faced by banking organizations involved with the programs. Sponsoring banking organizations generally face limited risk exposure to ABCP programs. This risk usually is confined to the credit enhancements and liquidity facility arrangements that sponsoring banking organizations provide to these programs.[210]

This language in the final rule demonstrates that regulators were blessing ABCP conduits—those entities typically set up by banks as SIVs off their balance sheets—as safe.[211]

That blessing is also consistent with what occurred prior to the 2004 rule. For years, federal banking regulators had allowed banks to create these SIVs as off–balance sheet assets so that banks could generate fees from insuring outside investors (such as MMFs) in ABCP.[212] It was good business for the banks, which were able to keep their capital charge low, and it provided added incentives for investors to buy ABCP. The data show that of all the ABCP conduits that were rated by Moody's Investors Service as of January 1, 2007, commercial banks sponsored more than half (52 percent) and funded nearly three-fourths of the total outstanding (74 percent).[213] Naturally, bank regulators knew that if the banks ever had to make good on those ABCP guarantees (i.e., support losses), the SIVs would have to be recognized and be taken back onto the balance sheet, requiring higher capital charges. That scenario, of course, is precisely the one that started unfolding in 2007.

Even if this rule change was not the main factor in the increased issuance of ABCP, it is demonstrably false that federal banking regulators were unaware of exactly how involved commercial banks were in the ABCP market. Moreover, banking regulators underestimated what the "limited"-risk exposure to ABSs meant for the banking sector. In fact, the overall performance of the risk-weighted capital framework that bank regulators implemented in 1988 has proven that regulators do not have superior knowledge over other market participants when it comes to measuring financial assets' risk.

Not only were these capital rules crafted on the basis of the "risk bucket" approach developed by the Federal Reserve in the 1950s, but the Fed (jointly with the FDIC and OCC) amended these rules in 2001 so that banks could hold even less capital for highly rated (privately issued) MBSs.[214] After the 2001 rule change, known as the *recourse rule*, certain AA- and AAA-rated ABSs were given the same low-risk weight (20 percent) as agency-issued MBSs. Evidence shows that the 10 largest U.S. banks expanded their purchases of these private-label MBSs and collateralized debt obligation (CDO) bonds as soon as the rule was changed. Even though these banks' assets doubled from 2001 to 2007, their risk-weight-adjusted assets barely increased.[215]

More broadly, the federal capital framework undoubtedly contributed to the buildup of all types of MBSs in the banking sector prior to the 2008 crisis because it provided financial incentives to sell mortgages and hold MBSs.[216] Thus, the federal framework has resulted in bank balance sheets becoming more uniform over time (banks now have a smaller number of more similar assets than in the past), thus placing more of the industry at risk to the same shocks. Combined, these failures suggest that the highly prescriptive bank regulations—touted as stability enhancing by proponents of stricter regulations in capital markets—may not have served the banking sector, or the broader economy, so well.

The evidence suggests that, in fact, regulators have not done a spectacular job at maintaining stability in the banking sector as they expanded regulations, a finding that holds internationally. In the preface to their 2014 book *Fragile by Design*, Charles Calomiris and Stephen Haber state that the book was released "after the worst three decades of banking crises the world has ever seen."[217] The authors title their first chapter "If Stable and Efficient Banks Are Such a Good Idea, Why Are They So Rare?"[218] They go on to make the case that systemic banking crises "do not happen without warning" and that "they occur when banking systems are made vulnerable by construction, as the result of political choices."[219] Among 115 developed nations, between 1970 and 2010, only 34 countries were crisis free, 62 had one financial crisis, and 19—including the United States—had two crises.[220]

Given that modern banking regulation displays this type of overall track record on stability, it is difficult to see how forcing more banklike regulations on capital markets could achieve financial stability.[221] Indeed, contrary to the conventional narrative, the evidence suggests that too much government involvement and regulation in the banking sector caused—and worsened—the 2008 crisis. At best, that prescriptive federal framework failed to prevent the crisis or the turmoil specific to the banking sector.[222]

Combined with the fact that there is essentially no evidence to support the 2008 contagion story, the case for expanding banklike regulation and government oversight to capital markets is incredibly weak. Nonetheless, after 2008, government officials relied heavily on the conventional crisis story to expand the federal regulatory framework by forcing more banklike regulations on certain nonbank financial firms. Unsurprisingly, the Biden administration is repeating that strategy.

6

MMF RULES: STEADILY SHIFTING IN THE WRONG DIRECTION

Relying on the conventional story about the 2008 financial crisis, the SEC finalized new MMF rules in both 2010 and 2014. Overall, these rule changes were not a success, because they failed to create the stable MMF industry that supporters envisioned and because they drastically reduced the funds available for financing commercial activity. In 2021, the SEC proposed yet another set of MMF rule changes, partly acknowledging the failures of the previous amendments. Despite the shortcomings of the 2010 and 2014 rule changes, the new rules likely satisfied many banking regulators, a group that has always had a somewhat tendentious relationship with MMFs.

In 1981, for instance, Fed Chairman Paul Volcker testified before a congressional committee that the Fed would prefer that "money market funds be subject to regulations that would make them more competitive with banking institutions and less attractive to investors."[223] Volcker proposed that Congress give MMFs reserve requirements, as well as rules that prevented investors from redeeming their shares on demand.[224] In 2009, Volcker counseled the Obama administration that "banks remain the functioning heart of the financial system, and they are protected and regulated," and to the extent that banks have competitors with "different ground rules," it "weakens the financial system."[225] In 2012, Treasury Secretary Timothy Geithner chastised the SEC for failing to implement stricter MMF regulations and urged the newly created FSOC to formally recommend that the SEC put new MMF rules into effect. Ultimately, those FSOC recommendations included proposals such as a floating net asset value (NAV), a NAV capital buffer, a separate capital/reserve requirement, and a provision requiring funds to withhold 3 percent of a shareholder's redemptions from any accounts over $100,000.[226]

As discussed in previous chapters, multiple government reports justify these types of regulations by arguing that MMFs exhibited an inherent vulnerability to destabilizing runs during the 2008 crisis. Nonetheless, MMFs have displayed such an excellent safety record that many of the same government reports—as well as other government agencies and research reports—have had no choice but to acknowledge it. For example, the 2010 PWG report concedes that in "the twenty-seven years since the adoption of [the SEC's] rule 2a-7, only two MMFs have broken the buck. In 1994, a small MMF suffered a capital loss because of exposures to interest rate derivatives, but the event passed without significant repercussions."[227] The report also states that although "the run on MMFs in 2008 is itself unique in the history of the industry, the events of 2008 underscored the susceptibility of MMFs to runs."[228] Naturally, the uniqueness of the 2008 run suggests that MMFs are not inherently susceptible to such problems. Likewise, a 2010 Federal Reserve paper notes that from "the introduction of the rules specifically governing these funds in 1983 until the Lehman bankruptcy in September 2008, only one small MMF lost money for investors," and even though "MMF prospectuses and advertisements must warn that 'it is possible to lose money by investing in the Fund,' investors virtually never lost anything."[229]

Although it may be surprising, basic evidence from the 2008 crisis demonstrates that even the turmoil in the MMF sector during that period did not result in major losses for shareholders. Of the more than 800 MMFs that existed at the end of 2007, only one broke the buck during the crisis.[230] Moreover, the shareholders of that fund—the now-infamous Reserve Primary Fund—ultimately received more than $0.98 on the dollar.[231] According to the conventional narrative, this success rate resulted only because the federal government stepped in to guarantee MMFs in 2008. A major problem with that theory, however, is that the Treasury guarantee program was never called on to cover *any* losses, a remarkable fact given that the program required participating funds to have a NAV greater than or equal to $0.995 and to liquidate if their share price fell by only one-half of a percent.[232]

In contrast, even though the FDIC's transaction account guarantee program provided unlimited insurance for $1.4 trillion in deposits, 140 banks failed in 2009, 160 failed in 2010, and an additional 108 failed in 2011 (plus the first quarter of 2012).[233] In fact, the long-term track record for federally insured banks is much worse than for MMFs; since 1970, federal assistance was provided to 593 depository institutions, and 3,028 institutions failed, at a cost to taxpayers of more than $180 billion.[234] Proponents of stricter MMF regulation also argue that because many fund sponsors stepped in to support share values by purchasing assets at par and waiting to resell them, the damage in the MMF industry was much worse than it appeared.[235] A major problem with this argument, though, is that MMFs were explicitly designed with such sponsor support mechanisms in mind, meaning that they worked exactly as they were supposed to work.[236] It should be very rare that an MMF would ever return less than $1 per share to its shareholders, and indeed it has seldom happened.

Despite the track record of MMFs and the lack of evidence for MMF contagion in 2008, the federal government moved ahead with two rounds of major MMF rule changes after the crisis. The FSOC recommended various new regulations in 2010 and 2012, and the SEC finalized new rules in 2010 and 2014, all of which were based on the idea that MMFs were inherently susceptible to destabilizing runs. The following list summarizes how MMFs were regulated prior to 2008 and provides an overview of how the rules were changed.

Original (1983) MMF Rules

The SEC regulates MMFs under the Investment Company Act of 1940, and it promulgated its first MMF rule in 1983. The rule, known as rule 2a-7, was concerned mostly with risk-limiting restrictions and the valuation of an MMF's shares.[237] Originally, the risk-limiting restrictions were relatively straightforward. For instance, MMFs were required to maintain an average portfolio maturity of less than or equal to 120 days, the maximum maturity for individual securities in the portfolio was one year, and the fund could purchase only bonds with one of the top two ratings from a major rating service.[238] The share valuation rules, however, have been the source of much debate and misinformation. For all mutual funds, the NAV of the fund represents the fund's per-share market value. In the case of a mutual fund that invests in a portfolio of publicly traded stocks, it is very easy to calculate the fund's NAV at the end of every day (the market value of the stocks, less any liabilities, divided by the outstanding shares). A problem for MMFs, even if they did not try to maintain a stable $1 NAV—which they all do try to achieve—is that they invest in many liquid assets (such as commercial paper and certificates of deposit) that do not regularly trade in a secondary market. That is, they invest in assets whose market prices are not regularly displayed and objectively reported (there is, for example, no exchange that lists closing prices). Because the value of those assets may fluctuate—though, in general, the value would not be expected to change much—calculation of the NAV for an MMF necessarily requires some estimation. As a result, rule 2a-7 required the MMF board to "establish procedures for maintaining a stable NAV using either the penny-rounding or amortized cost method" and further required any board using the amortized cost method "to monitor the deviation between the fund's NAV 'calculated using available market quotations (or an appropriate sub-stitute which reflects current market conditions)' and its amortized cost value per share."[239] Although proponents of requiring MMFs to report a floating (as opposed to fixed) NAV have suggested that the amortized cost method is an "accounting gimmick" that somehow results in "fictitious" pricing, it is a widely used valuation method for short-term debt securities that otherwise have no objectively reported market price.[240] Even requiring MMFs to use a floating NAV would necessitate that fund managers use some type of estimation procedure to price their portfolio unless they invest only in assets commonly traded in secondary markets.

MMF Rules in Place as of the 2008 Crisis

The SEC has amended rule 2a-7 multiple times since 1983, often changing the risk-limiting provisions in some way. At the time of the 2008 crisis, the version of rule 2a-7 that was in place followed the same general concept as the original rule. That is, the SEC allowed MMFs to report a stable NAV ($1 per share) provided that the value of the fund's shares remained within a narrow band around $1 and that the fund adhered to various risk-limiting restrictions. Specifically, the version of rule 2a-7 in force during 2008 limited the fund's average portfolio maturity to 90 days and generally prohibited investments in securities with maturities longer than 397 days. The rule also prohibited MMFs "from investing more than five percent of total assets in first tier [highest rated] securities from a single issuer," from "investing more than one percent of total assets (or $1 million, whichever was greater) in second tier securities of a single issuer," and from investing more than 5 percent of a fund's total assets in second-tier securities.[241]

2010 Amendments

The 2008 financial crisis led to many regulatory changes for MMFs, with the SEC finalizing one set of rule amendments in 2010.[242] According to the SEC, these rule changes were "designed to reduce the interest rate, liquidity, and credit risks of money market fund portfolios and, therefore, make money market funds less likely to break the buck."[243] Among other changes, the 2010 amendments lowered MMFs' maximum average portfolio maturity from 90 to 60 days and also added a new *weighted average life* requirement of 120 days, with the intent of limiting an MMF's ability to invest in longer-term floating rate securities. Additionally, the SEC imposed the following liquidity requirements: all taxable MMFs must hold at least 10 percent of assets in cash, U.S. Treasury securities, or securities that convert into cash (i.e., mature) within one day; and all MMFs must hold at least 30 percent of assets in cash, U.S. Treasury securities, or other short-term securities that convert into cash within one week. Separately, the rule restricted MMFs from holding illiquid securities (defined as any security that cannot be sold or disposed of within seven days at its carrying value) if "after the purchase, more than 5 percent of the fund's portfolio will be illiquid securities (rather than the current limit of 10 percent)."[244] The 2010 rules also imposed the following liquidity requirements: an MMF cannot invest more than 3 percent of its assets in second-tier securities (a decrease from 5 percent), cannot invest more than 0.5 percent of its assets in second-tier securities issued by any single issuer (the rule previously set a limit of the greater of 1 percent or $1 million), and cannot invest in second-tier securities that mature in more than 45 days (a decrease from 397 days).[245] The SEC implemented another major change under section 22(e) of the Investment Company Act, a provision of the law that generally prohibits mutual funds from suspending share redemptions except in certain limited circumstances. The 2010 amendments allowed the fund's board to suspend redemption if "the board, including a majority of the disinterested directors, (1) determines that 'the extent of the deviation between the fund's amortized cost price per share and its [market-based] current net asset value per share . . . may result in material dilution or other unfair results to investors or existing shareholders,' and (2) has irrevocably approved the fund's liquidation."[246] While the new maturity requirements surely had some influence on MMFs' portfolios, the precise relationship is not obvious. According to the Investment Company Institute, the average maturity for all U.S.-registered prime MMFs was 44 days in both 2007 and 2010; it was 40 days in 2011 and 45 days in 2012.[247] Moreover, it is unclear how much safer these rules made MMF portfolios. The data show, for example, a small increase in MMFs' portfolio share of various government securities and a large increase in certificates of deposit (from 15.2 percent of total assets in 2007 to 29.5 percent of total assets in 2012). Both the various federal securities and the bank certificates of deposit are, of course, ultimately backed by the federal government.

2014 Amendments

After the 2010 amendments, the SEC adopted more changes for rule 2a-7. According to the SEC, these amendments, proposed in 2014 and implemented in 2016, were based on the theory that the 2010 amendments did too little to address large-scale MMF redemptions.[248] Most of the amendments in this round of rulemaking were more controversial than the SEC's previous regulations. For instance, the 2014 amendments require MMF boards to choose between imposing a liquidity fee of up to 2 percent or suspending share redemptions (closing a "gate") if the fund's weekly liquid assets fall below 30 percent of the fund's total assets. The 2014 amendments also require the MMF board to impose a 1 percent liquidity fee if the fund's weekly liquid assets fall below 10 percent of total assets unless the board determines that doing so would not be in the best interest of the fund. The rule limits the gate to suspending redemptions for no more than 10 days. These gate and fee requirements do not, however, apply to any government MMF (one that invests 99.5 percent of its total assets in cash or government securities). The 2014 rules also implemented a major change to the way MMFs report their NAVs. First, all prime and tax-exempt institutional (as opposed to retail) MMFs were prohibited from using the amortized cost method of valuation and required to report a floating (rather than fixed) NAV to the nearest one-hundredth of a percent. Aside from the dubious implication that institutional investors must not be able to comprehend that the value of some assets in their MMF portfolio are being estimated, evidence from Europe (where funds are issued by using both fixed and floating NAVs) shows that the pricing method has no effect on share redemptions.[249] Regardless, the 2014 amendments caused a massive shift out of prime MMFs: shareholders moved more than $1 trillion into government MMFs ahead of the effective date (2016), dwarfing any of the outflows from prime MMFs during the 2008 crisis.[250] The portfolio composition of all taxable MMFs also changed dramatically ahead of 2016. In 2015, these funds' aggregate average portfolio share of government-backed or government securities was 15 percent, and their share of commercial paper was 15 percent. By December 2016, the MMFs' share of government-backed or government securities was up to 88 percent, and their commercial paper share was down to 4 percent.[251] To the extent that these rule changes were made ultimately to ensure that investment funds would be available to finance commercial activity, the amendments failed miserably.

2021 Proposed Rules

On December 15, 2021, the SEC proposed new amendments to the MMF rules, partly because of market activity during the COVID-19 pandemic.[252] In what amounts to an admission that the 2014 gate and fee provisions, with their explicit thresholds, increased the incentive to redeem shares, the SEC is now proposing to "remove the liquidity fee and redemption gate provisions in the existing rule, which would eliminate an incentive for preemptive redemptions from certain money market funds."[253] The proposal would also restrict the way funds use gates and fees, limiting their application to funds that are liquidating and also capping the fees at 2 percent.[254] Separately, the proposal would require institutional prime and tax-exempt MMFs to implement *swing pricing*, a policy that requires a fund manager to adjust the fund's NAV (up or down) to better ensure that investors who redeem their shares bear the liquidity costs.[255] The new proposal also seeks to increase MMFs' daily and weekly liquid asset requirements to 25 and 50 percent, respectively. Under the current rules, MMFs must hold at least 10 percent of their assets in daily liquid assets and at least 30 percent in weekly liquid assets. Given that both the existing and the proposed requirements would allow funds to invest in cash, government securities with multiple maturities, or other types of short-term investments, provided that they mature within the required number of days (one to five business days),[256] and since MMFs have already shifted their portfolio composition toward government securities, it is unclear what the marginal effect of these new daily and weekly liquid asset requirements might be.

The financial market stress that occurred during the COVID-19 pandemic and the subsequent government shutdowns is a primary driver of the latest MMF rules. As in previous downturns, federal regulators pointed to MMF share redemptions as a problem because they result in fewer funds being available to finance business activity in the private sector. For instance, the 2020 PWG report laments that between March 10 and 24, MMFs "cut their

CP [commercial paper] holdings by $35 billion," a reduction that represents "74 percent of the $48 billion overall decline in outstanding CP over those two weeks."[257] Aside from the fact that it would make sense for businesses to finance less activity during the shutdowns, the PWG report ignores that March 18—the date that the Federal Reserve created its MMF Liquidity Facility (MMLF)—falls squarely in the middle of the period the report analyzes.

According to the Fed, the MMLF was designed to purchase commercial paper from MMFs to enhance "overall market functioning and credit provision to the broader economy."[258] Obviously, if helping MMFs shed their commercial paper is beneficial to the broader economy, then when MMFs reduce their holdings on their own it cannot also be a cause of stress, an amplifier of stress, or some type of problem that requires new rules to prevent MMFs from selling their assets. Regardless, data show that "two-thirds of the reduction in prime funds' commercial paper holdings cited by the PWG—$23 billion of the $35 billion—occurred after the Fed's announcement and was driven by funds' sales of commercial paper that were ultimately pledged to the facility."[259] Moreover, it is difficult to see how MMFs' commercial paper sales could not have been at least partially driven by efforts to keep their weekly liquid assets above the thresholds that would have required them to implement gates and fees.

What happened to MMFs in 2020 is just the latest example of prescriptively designed rules and regulations that fail to work as the designers intend. Just as decades of increasingly strict bank regulations have failed to produce financial stability, so too have increasingly strict MMF rules. The failure of the recent MMF rule amendments even led to one of the harmful scenarios that was supposedly so dangerous in the first place, namely, reducing the funds available to finance commercial activity. Rather than acknowledge the failure of this top-down regulatory approach in short-term capital markets, the SEC's 2021 rule proposal doubles down with even more prescriptive rules, such as mandatory swing pricing and explicit restrictions on how funds can use fees and gates.

A better alternative would use the 1983 regulatory framework for MMFs as a baseline. From there, the SEC should pare down the prescriptive rules to the bare minimum, so that they include little more than an average maturity restriction. Rather than trying to improve financial markets by saddling MMFs with more operating restrictions, the SEC should allow fund managers and investors to figure out what works best for them. This approach would foster more competition in short-term credit markets and make them more resilient by decreasing the uniformity of investment options.

If some MMF investors want more risk, with a greater proportion of their funds invested in longer-duration money market securities, and if others want less risk, then the SEC should foster more such options with a flexible framework based on preventing fraud and promoting transparency. As George Mason University professor Larry White recently observed, "The goal of a robust financial system calls for a diverse ecosystem of mutual funds, not a monoculture that is susceptible to a single disease. Top-down restrictions promote a monoculture."[260] Given regulators' track record, it makes sense that fund managers and shareholders, not federal officials, should shoulder the responsibility of figuring out what investment structures provide the right incentives and options. Still, proponents of stricter regulation disagree with this approach. They favor instead an expansive—virtually limitless—federal role in financial market regulation.

7

SYSTEMIC RISK REGULATION AND STABILITY: THE NEVER-ENDING STORY

Many government officials, industry participants, and academics endorse an extensive federal role for financial regulation, one that requires regulators to promote financial stability by addressing systemic risks.[261] This approach requires regulators to address known threats to financial stability as well as potential threats to stability.[262] Much of the 2010 Dodd-Frank Act reflects this approach, one that relies on the conventional story about the 2008 financial crisis. For instance, a recent report coauthored by several academic scholars and former government officials states that "nonbank intermediation and banking share very similar financial stability risks—contagion across institutions and markets resulting in runs of short-term funding and associated *asset fire sales* [emphasis added] that impede the delivery of essential services to households and businesses."[263]

There are several problems with this regulatory approach. As discussed previously, the conventional story about the 2008 financial crisis does not justify an expansive federal role for regulating financial markets, largely because the evidence shows that federal rules and regulations were a primary cause of the crisis. Similarly, the specific claim that asset fire sales contribute to market turmoil ignores the role that the federal legal and regulatory frameworks play in financial firms' decisions to sell assets during a crisis. Much like the evidence for broader contagion, the evidence for contagious fire sales during the 2008 crisis often makes a case against more government regulation.

The concept of asset fire sales, which also surfaces in the SEC's newly proposed MMF rules,[264] is a specific type of contagion whereby the rush to sell certain assets can depress their prices as well as the prices of other assets. But it's not just the actual fire sales that concern regulators; it's also the risk: as a 2013 Federal Reserve report states, "*The risk* [emphasis added] of 'fire sales,' , . . . is a major source of financial instability."[265] Never mind, for now, whether it makes sense to allow regulators the discretion required to guard against potential threats to financial stability;[266] evaluation of the research findings regarding asset fire sales during the 2008 crisis is fairly straightforward.

For instance, the 2013 Federal Reserve report cited in the previous paragraph examines the risk of fire sales in the tri-party repo market during 2007–2009. The paper states that "the risk of fire sales is a particularly acute concern in the tri-party repo market because of the size of dealers' portfolios and the strong incentives for some lenders to sell collateral quickly in a default event."[267] The paper describes the well-documented stress in the repo market during the 2008 crisis and acknowledges that "many tri-party repo lenders face operational or regulatory constraints that create strong incentives to liquidate assets."[268] In other words, the potential problem for the dealers is caused, or at least exacerbated, by regulatory and legal constraints, both of which provide strong incentives (and in some cases requirements) to sell securities to increase liquidity. The resulting decline in repo financing, supposedly, can threaten not just these dealers, but the broader economy as well.

While the paper does not study the effects that asset fire sales can have beyond the repo market, it does provide two citations for "empirical evidence on fire sales."[269] One of the cited works studies the market for nonagency residential mortgage-backed securities (RMBS) during 2006–2009 and finds that "the combination of capital requirements and fair value accounting rules" is a primary cause of insurance companies' decisions to sell low-quality assets at fire sale prices.[270] The study examines data for insurance companies, but the authors also note, "While capital requirements for U.S. banks were not credit-quality sensitive for loans, they were for structured finance securities such as RMBS, so that we would expect the issues raised in this paper to be relevant for RMBS transactions by banks as well."[271]

A second study of the institutional bond market finds that "when the [2008 financial] crisis hit the securitized bond market, the shock was transmitted by the portfolio decisions of institutional investors, which held both securitized bonds and corporate bonds and had to liquidate portions of their portfolios due to their liquidity needs."[272] Similar to what happened in other markets, the evidence shows that regulatory requirements also drove these firms' decisions to sell certain types of bonds. The authors conclude:

> Mutual funds did not rush to sell the now illiquid securitized bonds en masse, but, instead, sharply reduced their holdings of corporate bonds. The insurance companies, in contrast, sold neither class of assets (except those with a below-threshold level of risk-based capital, which reduced holdings of securitized bonds). In addition, funds

with negative contemporaneous flows, high turnover, or high flow volatility liquidated greater portions of their corporate bond holdings than other funds, behavior suggesting that their portfolio decisions were dominated by liquidity needs. Interestingly, the average mutual fund tended to sell more junk bonds than investment-grade bonds.[273]

Thus, in this scenario, much like other contagion studies, the authors report that stark differences across intermediaries, rather than a general panic, drove decisions to sell assets.

Proponents of stricter regulations could, of course, argue that the absence of a general panic is irrelevant and that regulators need to protect the financial system from asset fire sales. One problem with that argument, though, is that the regulatory and legal frameworks are key causal factors behind the decision to sell the assets in the first place, and there is no inherent reason to think that regulators have any special ability to determine beforehand the best way to restrict sales of certain assets in the event of market turmoil. Thus, removal of these incentives to sell assets into a declining market would necessitate removal of the prescriptive regulations that subjectively apply regulators' risk standards to certain types of assets.

More broadly, this regulatory approach—requiring regulators to reduce systemic risks by regulating both known and potential threats to financial stability—is theoretically flawed because its goal is to ensure that financial firms continue to provide credit even in market downturns.[274] It gives no consideration to whether economic fundamentals dictate that a slowdown of some kind is warranted, so that financial firms should provide less financing. Both in theory and in practice, this approach requires the federal government to prevent certain investors from taking (at least some) losses, thus transferring wealth from taxpayers who absorb the losses to those who originally took the financial risks.

In addition to reducing economic efficiency and redistributing wealth, this approach also increases market participants' incentives to lobby for rules and regulations that help protect their interests, thus increasing the chances that firms will take on "too much" risky behavior. This result empowers a small group of bureaucrats to collude with well-connected industry participants, ultimately allowing them to dictate economic decisions for everyone else on the basis of increasingly broad and subjective criteria. There is essentially no limit to how restrictive federal regulators can be because they merely need to describe any possible occurrence as a potential threat to stability. In any economy based on individual rights and limited government, the goal of the regulatory framework should not be to reduce the risk of failure to certain financial firms or to the broader system because such a framework undermines both individual rights and a limited government.

Some proponents of expansive systemic risk regulation ignore this critique and instead argue that the regulatory approach is necessary to protect the banking system because commercial bank deposits are federally insured. This argument takes several forms, ranging from protecting the FDIC deposit insurance fund to preventing noninsured financial firms from receiving subsidies. Cornell law professor Saule Omarova, for example, posits that "it may be more effective to manage the safety and soundness of depository institutions through legal and regulatory mechanisms aimed at ensuring stability of the entire financial system"[275] and then argues for strengthening Section 23A of the Federal Reserve Act. Specifically, she claims (as do several legal scholars) that one of the main purposes of Section 23A—a purpose which, in her view, has not been adequately fulfilled—is to prevent a transfer "of federal subsidy (access to federal deposit insurance and liquidity backup facilities)" to nonbank financial firms.[276]

These arguments are not persuasive for multiple reasons. First, Section 23A of the Federal Reserve Act does restrict the types of transactions that depository institutions may engage in with their affiliated companies, but it does not provide a regulatory mandate for the Fed to prevent the transfer of any kind of federal subsidy to affiliated (or nonaffiliated) nonbank firms, even if one reads Section 23A broadly. In practice, such a restriction would be virtually meaningless because any insured depository institution that uses the Fed's facilities and then lends to other firms effectively passes on (at least some of) any related federal subsidy. Moreover, neither Section 23A nor any other federal statute gives the *Federal Reserve* an explicit mandate to protect the FDIC deposit insurance fund, and contrary arguments appear to be based on the desire to expand the reach of the Federal Reserve.

Federally chartered banks are supervised by the OCC, and state-chartered banks that are not members of the Federal Reserve system are regulated by the FDIC.[277] There is no inherent reason that either the OCC or the FDIC could not regulate banks to ensure the safety of the FDIC deposit insurance fund, and it makes little sense to argue that the Federal Reserve must also regulate these banks. Additionally, policymakers should not assume that only the federal government can provide banks with deposit insurance,[278] and they should acknowledge that prescriptive banking regulations (based on mitigating systemic risks or otherwise) have failed to protect the banking system.

Historically, the federal government has found it increasingly difficult to avoid bailing out large financial institutions that took excessive risk, and virtually every sort of crisis has been met with added federal regulation in the name of preventing the next calamity. This approach has yet to work. Rather than forcing financial firms to adhere to more arbitrary standards set by regulatory fiat, policymakers should reduce prescriptive regulations and introduce more market discipline into the system. This approach can be implemented by, for example, alleviating the Federal Reserve of its regulatory responsibilities and implementing a regulatory framework based on promoting transparent disclosure and discouraging fraud. A less prescriptive regulatory framework will not guarantee a more stable financial system, but a highly prescriptive framework has already been proven to produce a fragile system.

CONCLUSION

The National Bureau of Economic Research estimates that the United States has had 34 recessions since 1854, and only 7 lasted longer than the 2007–2009 recession. Since the Great Depression, no downturn has lasted longer. Five other recessions, all prior to the 1930s, matched the 18-month duration. Though many policymakers argue that the 2007–2009 recession would have been worse without so much federal intervention, there is good reason to doubt the success of the federal government's efforts, particularly those related to mitigating the 2008 financial crisis. In fact, without such extensive previous government intervention, the crisis would likely have been much less severe, if it had occurred at all.

As this book has demonstrated, the conventional story about the 2008 crisis portrays the federal government's crisis mitigation efforts as heroic and blames capitalism—in the unregulated shadow banking sector—for excessive exotic financial bets that roiled markets and cratered the economy. The problem with this story is that it ignores much of reality. It disregards, for example, that federal rules and regulations provided many incentives to issue and hold the types of ABSs at the center of the financial meltdown. It also rejects the fact that most of that financial activity—and asset securitization in general—took place within the traditional banking sector, with the explicit blessing of federal banking regulators. Finally, it ignores the differences between investors reacting to economic stress and investors causing economic stress.

It is one thing to ignore these aspects of reality, but to then insist, on the grounds of a false narrative, on imposing banklike regulations on the nonbank firms operating in capital markets defies reason. Historically, the increasingly paternalistic and prescriptive federal regulatory framework has destabilized the banking sector and nonbank financial markets. There is no reason to believe that expanding this approach to more short-term capital intermediaries will do anything other than produce the same harmful outcomes, only more broadly. After roughly one century of ratcheting up this approach, the results clearly show that federal regulators do not have superior knowledge over others when it comes to measuring financial assets' risk. Regardless of how comforting it might be to think that regulators can finally develop the right set of rules, the one that will keep markets stable, that notion is a fantasy that ignores the costs of implementing such a framework.

The truth is that government officials cannot design vibrant capital markets that are always perfectly stable if they also want to allow investors to take the risks that create vibrant capital markets. That the common good depends on these types of regulations is merely an emotional appeal, one that ignores how much the traditional regulatory approach has harmed both the common good and individual rights. Continued attempts to create such a perfectly stable environment will further weaken financial markets by giving investors even fewer choices and by more heavily concentrating risks.

The best way to promote stable financial markets is with policies that foster a diverse set of investment types and intermediaries, so that people can appropriately diversify their own risk from a broader set of choices. A rigid prescriptive framework creates a monoculture with fewer investment options, making it more difficult to balance risks across multiple types of assets. It creates an inherently fragile system, ultimately undercutting the ability of the free enterprise system—which is based on economic freedom—to help people prosper and live productive and happy lives.

Few policymakers in Washington, DC, even question the conventional crisis story, much less advocate the connection between economic freedom and financial markets' health. Instead, most use that narrative to justify the expansive financial regulations put in place after the crisis and to promote even more banklike regulations and federal backing for short-term credit markets. The Biden administration, for example, is using the conventional story to justify new rules for MMFs as well as for *stablecoins*, financial instruments that did not even exist during the 2008 financial crisis. Multiple other government officials use elements of the standard explanation of the 2008 crisis to push for more-expansive systemic risk regulations, especially outside the banking sector. However, the record shows that the conventional story about the 2008 crisis does not justify this approach.

The MMF rules that the SEC implemented in 2010 and 2014 provide an excellent recent case study. These regulations, supposedly necessary to fix structural vulnerabilities in MMFs that made them inherently unstable, caused even larger outflows from the private sector to the government sector than those experienced during the 2008 crisis. It also became clear in 2020 that the rules failed to achieve their stated purpose of stopping the incentive to redeem shares during economic turmoil. Astonishingly, many federal officials still want to double down on this failed regulatory approach by implementing increasingly prescriptive rules in existing markets as well as new market segments. Thus, it does appear that the conventional 2008 crisis narrative has taken hold and is firmly rooted in the psyche of federal officials.

Nonetheless, this book has provided a comprehensive account of the 2008 financial crisis and demonstrated that the conventional explanation is false. That story does not provide a solid rationale for spreading more banklike regulations to the rest of the financial markets. The following list summarizes the main arguments in this book:

- The conventional story about the 2008 financial crisis is highly misleading, for several reasons.
- Contagion—infectious runs that indiscriminately propagate throughout financial markets and the broader economy—was not the primary driver of the 2008 crisis.
- There is an astonishing lack of empirical evidence to support the contagion hypothesis and a great deal of evidence that contradicts it.
- There is sufficient evidence to doubt that contagion caused the run on the Reserve Primary Fund to spread to the rest of the MMF sector or that it caused turmoil to spread from MMFs to other short-term credit markets.
- Short-term credit markets did not freeze during the 2008 crisis. New issues of commercial paper

and repos became more expensive, frequently for shorter maturities and often requiring alternative forms of collateral (instead of the ABSs that had been used), but these facts demonstrate that those markets worked as they should.

- Most commercial paper is issued only by very large companies with stellar credit ratings, firms that would otherwise have no trouble borrowing from banks, such as Ford, John Deere, and Citigroup. Historically, the nonfinancial commercial paper market has remained safe and stable, as it did during the 2008 financial crisis.

- Leading up to the 2008 crisis, most ABCP was sold to outside investors with explicit bank-provided guarantees that required commercial banks to pay off maturing ABCP at full face value in the event of a default.

- The repo market is dominated by large securities dealers, firms that include the Federal Reserve's primary dealers. U.S. Treasury securities are the most common collateral in the repo market by far, with agency debt and MBSs a close second, such that approximately 70 percent of the collateral used in the repo market consists of government-backed securities.

- Unlike commercial banks, MMFs generally are not leveraged (they do not invest borrowed funds), but an increasing number of commercial banks have sponsored MMFs since the 1980s.

- Bank-sponsored prime institutional MMFs accounted for more than half of all prime institutional MMF assets by the end of 2007. Banks provide explicit guarantees for their conduits that create

MMFs, as for commercial paper, thus increasing the liabilities for the commercial banking sector.

- Both nonbanks and commercial banks were heavily involved in asset securitization since that market began, and federal regulators were always aware of banks' involvement. From 1990 to 2008, commercial banks' market share for the principal functions of securitization (including issuing, trustee services, underwriting, and servicing) remained well over 90 percent.

- Even most of the so-called exotic financial instruments that gained notoriety during the 2008 crisis, such as the CDSs, the CDOs, and the SIVs, were developed by commercial banks. At least as early as 1991, federal regulators considered new regulations for these instruments.

- Blaming the shadow banks for the turmoil during the 2008 financial crisis is highly misleading because commercial banks were heavily involved with commercial paper, repos, securitization, and MMFs.

- None of this shadow banking activity took place in the shadows. Almost all of it took place directly through either a commercial bank or an affiliate of a Federal Reserve–regulated bank holding company. It unequivocally occurred in the purview of federal banking regulators. Indeed, it could have occurred only with their explicit blessing.

- Even though it may be difficult to believe given the pervasiveness of the conventional story about the 2008 crisis, many prime MMFs gained assets around the time of the Lehman failure and the Reserve Primary Fund's breaking of the buck.

- Empirical evidence shows that declines in the ABCP market negatively affected commercial banks but that those losses did not transfer to outside investors.

- Even if government guarantee programs can have a positive effect on stability during a crisis, such government intervention also can have negative effects, including some that are not immediately recognized during the crisis, such as a long-term shift away from providing capital to private businesses.

- Evidence suggests that regulatory policies designed to minimize the probability of runs on prime MMFs would do little to mitigate a broader financial crisis.

- The conventional story of the 2008 crisis essentially ignores all the economic and financial problems that surfaced in 2006 and 2007. It one-sidedly attributes credit market difficulties to a handful of events in 2008, such as Lehman's failure or the run on the Reserve Primary Fund.

- The evidence suggests that Reserve Primary Fund shareholders—and other prime MMF investors—redeemed shares because of the economic and financial problems, as well as the confusing government interventions, that occurred leading up to September 2008. That is, these investors reacted to market turmoil; they did not cause it.

- The supposed success of the federal interventions during the 2008 crisis ignores, among other things, the piecemeal fashion in which the federal government escalated its efforts after previous interventions had failed to end the turmoil.

- Of the more than 800 MMFs that existed at the end of 2007, only one broke the buck during the crisis, and the Reserve Primary Fund's shareholders ultimately received more than $0.98 cents on the dollar. In contrast, the FDIC's TAG program provided unlimited insurance for $1.4 trillion in deposits, but 140 banks failed in 2009, 160 failed in 2010, and an additional 108 failed between January 2011 and March 2012.

- On March 18, 2020, the Federal Reserve created the MMLF. This new facility was designed to purchase commercial paper from MMFs to enhance "overall market functioning and credit provision to the broader economy." If helping MMFs shed their commercial paper is beneficial to the broader economy, the fact that MMFs reduced their holdings on their own, prior to the creation of the MMLF, could not also have been a cause or amplifier of stress.

NOTES

Chapter 1

1. According to a 2007 *Fortune* article by the founder of the investment management company PIMCO, "My PIMCO colleague Paul McCulley has labeled it the 'shadow banking system' because it has lain hidden for years, untouched by regulation, yet free to magically and mystically create and then package subprime loans into a host of three-letter conduits that only Wall Street wizards could explain." Bill Gross, "Beware Our Shadow Banking System," *Fortune*, November 28, 2007.

2. See Gary Gorton and Andrew Metrick, "Regulating the Shadow Banking System," *Brookings Papers on Economic Activity* (Fall 2010): 261–62.

3. Janet Yellen, "Improving the Oversight of Large Financial Institutions" (speech, Citizens Budget Commission, New York, March 3, 2015).

4. Ben S. Bernanke, chairman, Board of Governors of the Federal Reserve System, statement before the Financial Crisis Inquiry Commission Public Hearing on Too Big to Fail: Expectations and Impact of Extraordinary Government Intervention and the Role of Systemic Risk in the Financial Crisis, day 2, session 1, September 2, 2010.

5. Timothy F. Geithner, *Stress Test: Reflections on Financial Crises* (New York: Crown Publishers, 2014), pp. 195–96.

6. Geithner, *Stress Test*, p. 433.

7. Andrew Ross Sorkin, *Too Big to Fail: The Inside Story of How Wall Street and Washington Fought to Save the Financial System—and Themselves* (New York: Viking, 2009), p. 412.

8. Sorkin, *Too Big to Fail*, p. 413.

9. Morgan Ricks, *The Money Problem: Rethinking Financial Regulation* (Chicago: University of Chicago Press, 2016), p. 3.

10. Ricks, *The Money Problem*, p. 3.

11. Ricks, *The Money Problem*, p. 3.

12. Gregg Gelzinis, "Strengthening the Regulation and Oversight of Shadow Banks," Center for American Progress, July 18, 2019.

13. Corporate Finance Institute, "Shadow Banking System," last modified September 20, 2020.

14. Kimberly Amadeo, "Lehman Brothers Collapse," The Balance, May 31, 2021.

15. President's Working Group on Financial Markets, *Overview of Recent Events and Potential Reform Options for Money Market Funds* (Washington: PWG, December 2020), p. 4.

16. SEC, "Money Market Fund Reforms," Proposed Rule, 17 CFR Parts 270 and 274 (December 15, 2021), p. 10.

17. SEC, "Money Market Fund Reforms," p. 172.

18. Richard G. Anderson and Charles S. Gascon, "The Commercial Paper Market, the Fed, and the 2007–2009 Financial Crisis," Federal Reserve Bank of St. Louis *Review* (November/ December 2009): 589. Also see Richard T. Selden, "Four Decades of Change in the Commercial Paper Market," in *Trends and Cycles in the Commercial Paper Market*, ed. Richard T. Selden (Cambridge, MA: National Bureau of Economic Research, 1963), pp. 6–30.

19. Lloyd B. Thomas, *Money, Banking, and Financial Markets* (Mason, OH: Thomson/Southwestern, 2006), pp. 52–53. Research shows that, as of the 1990s, commercial paper was issued almost exclusively by firms with strong balance sheets and high cash flows and that issuing firms' balance sheets do not deteriorate in quality throughout the business cycle. Charles Calomiris, Charles Himmelberg, and Paul Wachtel, "Commercial Paper, Corporate Finance, and the Business Cycle: Microeconomic Perspective," *Carnegie-Rochester Conference Series on Public Policy*, 42 (1995): 205.

20. The short-term maturity is by choice of investors and issuers, not because of regulatory requirements. Anderson and Gascon, "The Commercial Paper Market."

21. Viral V. Acharya, Philipp Schnabl, and Gustavo Suarez, "Securitization without Risk Transfer," *Journal of Financial Economics* 107, no. 3 (March 2013): 519–20. https://doi.org/10.1016/j.jfineco.2012.09.004

22. Viktoria Baklanova, Isaac Kuznits, and Trevor Tatum, "Primer: Money Market Funds and the Commercial Paper Market," Division of Investment Management's Analytics Office of the U.S. Securities and Exchange Commission, November 9, 2020.

23. Acharya et al., "Securitization without Risk Transfer," p. 518; Federal Reserve Board of Governors, "Asset-Backed Commercial Paper Outstanding (ABCOMP)," retrieved January 6, 2022, from Federal Reserve Bank of St. Louis (FRED).

24. Viktoria Baklanova, Adam Copeland, and Rebecca McCaughrin, "Reference Guide to U.S. Repo and Securities Lending Markets," Federal Reserve Bank of New York Staff Report no. 740, September 2015, p. 5.

25. Norbert J. Michel, "Federal Reserve's Expansion of Repurchase Market Is a Bad Idea," Issue Brief no. 4261, Heritage Foundation, August 14, 2014.

26. "US Repo Markets: A Chart Book," Securities Industry and Financial Markets Association, 2022.

27. "What Types of Asset Are Used as Collateral in the Repo Market?," International Capital Markets Association, 2021; "US Repo Market Fact Sheet," 2022; "Repo Market Fact Sheet," Securities Industry and Financial Markets Association, 2014; and Viktoria Baklanova et al., "The U.S. Bilateral Repo Market: Lessons from a New Survey," Office of Financial Research Brief Series, January 13, 2016.

28. Thomas, *Money, Banking, and Financial Markets*, pp. 52–53; Baklanova et al., "Reference Guide to U.S. Repo and Securities Lending Markets."

29. Viktoria Baklanova, Isaac Kuznits, and Trevor Tatum, "Primer: Money Market Funds and the Repo Market," Division of Investment Management's Analytics Office of the U.S. Securities and Exchange Commission, February 18, 2021.

30. In both the tri-party and the bilateral repo market segments, some transactions are "cleared," meaning that the counterparties transfer risk to a third party (a clearing bank). See David Bowman et al., "The Cleared Bilateral Repo Market and Proposed Repo Benchmark Rates," *FEDS Notes*, February 27, 2017. https://doi.org/10.17016/2380-7172.1940

31. Investment Company Institute, *Report of the Money Market Working Group* (Washington: Investment Company Institute, March 17, 2009), p. 141.

32. Thomas, *Money, Banking, and Financial Markets*, pp. 81–84.

33. Baklanova et al., "Primer: Money Market Funds and the Commercial Paper Market."

34. Baklanova et al., "Primer: Money Market Funds and the Repo Market."

35. Baklanova et al., "Primer: Money Market Funds and the Repo Market."

36. Baklanova et al., "Primer: Money Market Funds and the Repo Market."

37. Baklanova et al., "Primer: Money Market Funds and the Repo Market."

38. Because of interest rate price controls in the banking sector, MMFs grew steadily throughout the 1970s, and Congress passed the Depository Institutions Deregulation Act of 1980 to phase out the interest rate caps by 1986. Congress also passed the Garn–St. Germain Depository Institutions Act in 1982, allowing depository institutions to offer money market deposit accounts that paid customers higher interest rates than those at the statutory caps. See Betty R. Turner, "Markets for Money—Does the Garn–St. Germain Money Market Deposit Account Overcompete with Mutual Funds?," *Vanderbilt Law Review* 36, no. 4 (May 1983): article 7.

39. Stefan Jacewitz and Haluk Unal, "Shadow Insurance? Money Market Fund Investors and Bank Sponsorship," Center for Financial Research Working Paper 2020-03, Federal Deposit Insurance Corporation, June 2020, p. 5.

40. Interestingly, Bernanke's statement to the Financial Crisis Inquiry Commission notes that "a large portion of the investments

of these [money market] funds were in short-term wholesale funding instruments issued or guaranteed by commercial banks." See Bernanke, statement before the Financial Crisis Inquiry Commission.

41. "Computer Leases Back Financing by Sperry," *New York Times*, February 12, 1985. Also see Alan P. Murray, "Has Securitization Increased Risk to the Financial System?," *Business Economics* 36, no. 1 (January 2001): 63–67.

42. Murray, "Has Securitization Increased Risk?," p. 63.

43. "Computer Leases Back Financing by Sperry," February 12, 1985.

44. Nicola Cetorelli and Stavros Peristiani, "The Role of Banks in Asset Securitization," *Federal Reserve Bank of New York Economic Policy Review* (July 2012): 58. Also see Melanie L. Fein, "The Shadow Banking Charade," working paper, February 15, 2013. https://dx.doi.org/10.2139/ssrn.2218812

45. Cetorelli and Peristiani, "The Role of Banks in Asset Securitization," 58.

46. See Fein, "The Shadow Banking Charade," pp. 48–73; Carrick Mollenkamp et al., "How London Created a Snarl in Global Markets," *Wall Street Journal*, October 18, 2007; and Gillian Tett, *Fool's Gold: How Unrestrained Greed Corrupted a Dream, Shattered Global Markets and Unleashed a Catastrophe* (New York: Free Press, 2009), pp. 23–71 and 97. As Tett explains, in the 1990s, the securitization vehicles known as credit default swaps (CDSs) and synthetic CDOs were created by employees of J. P. Morgan, and the structured investment vehicle (SIV) concept was pioneered at Citibank. At least as early as 1991, the New York Fed was considering new regulations for these derivative securities.

47. Several government reports have been careful to make this distinction and argue for using the term *market-based finance* rather than shadow banking. See, for example, U.S. Department of the Treasury, *A Financial System That Creates Economic Opportunities: Asset Management and Insurance*, October 2017, p. 63.

48. Gary B. Gorton, "Slapped in the Face by the Invisible Hand: The Panic of 2007," prepared for the Federal Reserve Bank of Atlanta's 2009 Financial Markets Conference: Financial Innovation and Crisis, May 11-13, 2009, p. 37.

49. Zoltan Pozsar et al., "Shadow Banking," Federal Reserve Bank of New York Staff Report no. 458, July 2010. The term is sometimes used to denote the nonbank financial firms that do not have direct access to the Federal Reserve's discount window, but that distinction ignores that the Fed was explicitly designed to provide liquidity to commercial banks so that they could continue lending to both nonfinancial and financial firms outside the banking sector. (It also ignores that the Fed has historically provided liquidity support to firms outside the banking sector. See Norbert J. Michel, "The Fed's Failure as a Lender of Last Resort: What to Do about It," Backgrounder no. 2943, Heritage Foundation, August 20, 2014.)

50. Although there has been a perceived separation between commercial banking and capital markets in the United States since the 1933 Glass-Steagall Act, the close connection between the banking and capital markets sectors is nothing new. In fact, one reason that the Glass-Steagall restrictions on commercial and investment banking were so theoretically flawed was that investment banks regularly borrowed from commercial banks to engage in the "speculative" activities that Senator Glass abhorred. Norbert J. Michel, "The Glass–Steagall Act: Unraveling the Myth," Backgrounder no. 3104, Heritage Foundation, April 28, 2016.

51. Michael D. Bordo, Angela Redish, and Hugh Rockoff, "Why Didn't Canada Have a Banking Crisis in 2008 (or in 1930, or 1907, or . . .)?," National Bureau of Economic Research Working Paper no. 17312, August 2011, pp. 2, 8, and 23–24.

Chapter 2

52. President's Working Group on Financial Markets, *Overview of Recent Events and Potential Reform Options for Money Market Funds,* p. 4. A Biden administration report on stablecoins uses the same logic to argue that stablecoins should be issued only by federally insured depository institutions. See President's Working Group on Financial Markets, the Federal Deposit Insurance Corporation, and the Office of the Comptroller of the Currency, *Report on Stablecoins* (Washington: U.S. Treasury Department, November 2021), p. 1.

53. President's Working Group on Financial Markets, *Overview of Recent Events and Potential Reform Options for Money Market Funds*, p. 4, footnote 4.

54. President's Working Group on Financial Markets, *Money Market Fund Reform Options* (Washington: PWG, October 2010), pp. 11–13.

55. President's Working Group on Financial Markets, *Money Market Fund Reform Options*, p. 8. Prime MMFs are those that invest in short-term securities *other than* Treasury and other federal agency securities.

56. FSOC, "Proposed Recommendations Regarding Money Market Mutual Fund Reform," November 2012, p. 4.

57. FSOC, "Proposed Recommendations," p. 17.

58. FSOC, "Proposed Recommendations," p. 17, footnote 24.

59. See Patrick McCabe, "The Cross Section of Money Market Fund Risks and Financial Crises," Finance and Economics Discussion Paper 2010-51, Divisions of Research & Statistics and Monetary Affairs, Federal Reserve Board, September 12, 2010. The 2012 FSOC report also references an empirical study published in 1994, one that studies MMF rule changes implemented in 1991. See Sean S. Collins and Phillip Mack, "Avoiding Runs in Money Market Mutual Funds: Have Regulatory Reforms Reduced the Potential for a Crash?," Finance and Economics Discussion Paper 94-14, Divisions of Research & Statistics and Monetary Affairs, Federal Reserve Board, June 1994.

60. The 2012 FSOC report also inadvertently provides evidence that government intervention (up to that point) *failed to stop* the turmoil in financial markets. It notes that "*despite* [emphasis added] government intervention, the run in September 2008 led to rapid disinvestment by MMFs of short-term instruments which severely exacerbated stress in already strained financial markets." FSOC, "Proposed Recommendations," p. 25.

61. FSOC, "Proposed Recommendations," p. 25.

62. FSOC, "Proposed Recommendations," pp. 25–26.

63. President's Working Group on Financial Markets, *Money Market Fund Reform Options*, p. 12.

64. Lawrence Schmidt, Allan Timmermann, and Russ Wermers, "Runs on Money Market Mutual Funds," *American Economic Review* 106, no. 9 (September 2016): 2625–57.

65. Schmidt et al. "Runs on Money Market Mutual Funds," 2652.

66. Schmidt et al., "Runs on Money Market Mutual Funds," 2652.

67. Other research confirms that similar so-called runs were not indiscriminate. For instance, Federal Reserve researchers argue that runs were not indiscriminate in the ABCP market and that "runs in the crisis instead were significantly more likely at riskier programs, based on observable program characteristics, program type, sponsor type, and macro-financial variables." See Daniel M. Covitz, Nellie Liang, and Gustavo A. Suarez, "The Evolution of a Financial Crisis: Collapse of the Asset-Backed Commercial Paper Market," *Journal of Finance* 68, no. 3 (June 2013): 818.

68. Division of Risk, Strategy, and Financial Innovation, *Response to Questions Posed by Commissioners Aguilar, Paredes, and Gallagher* (Washington: SEC, November 30, 2012), p. 7.

69. Anderson and Gascon, "The Commercial Paper Market" p. 590.

70. Following each of these periods of net decreases, the total outstanding amount of commercial paper never exceeded the level outstanding just prior to the decline, but sporadic aggregate increases still occurred. Similar patterns exist for the following subcategories of commercial paper: ABCP, nonfinancial commercial paper, and financial commercial paper. These figures refer to the following data series, all downloaded from FRED Economic Data, Federal Reserve Bank of St. Louis, December 8, 2021: Commercial Paper Outstanding, Billions of Dollars, Weekly, Seasonally Adjusted (COMPOUT); Asset-Backed Commercial Paper Outstanding, Billions of Dollars, Weekly, Seasonally Adjusted (ABCOMP); Nonfinancial Commercial Paper Outstanding, Billions of Dollars, Weekly, Not Seasonally Adjusted (COMPAPER); and Financial Commercial Paper Outstanding, Billions of Dollars, Weekly, Seasonally Adjusted (FINCP).

71. Covitz et al., "The Evolution of a Financial Crisis," 818.

72. Covitz et al., "The Evolution of a Financial Crisis," 818.

73. Acharya et al., "Securitization without Risk Transfer," 515–36.

74. Acharya et al., "Securitization without Risk Transfer," 515–36.

75. Acharya et al., "Securitization without Risk Transfer," 516.

76. Gary Gorton, Toomas Laarits, and Andrew Metrick, "The Run on Repo and the Fed's Response," *Journal of Financial Stability* 48 (2020): 2.

77. Gary B. Gorton, "Slapped in the Face," abstract.

78. Gorton, "Slapped in the Face," p. 31.

79. Gorton, "Slapped in the Face," p. 32.

80. Gorton, "Slapped in the Face," p. 32.

81. Gary Gorton and Andrew Metrick, "Securitized Banking and the Run on the Repo," National Bureau of Economic Research Working Paper no. 15223, August 2009, p. 1. An updated version of this paper was published in 2012 in the *Journal of Financial Economics*. This paper will be discussed further herein.

82. Gorton and Metrick, "Securitized Banking and the Run on the Repo," pp. 1–2.

83. Gorton, "Slapped in the Face," p. 36.

84. Bank for International Settlements, *BIS Quarterly Review*, International Banking and Financial Market Developments, December 2008.

85. Gara Afonso, Anna Kovner, and Antoinette Schoar, "Stressed, Not Frozen: The Federal Funds Market in the Financial Crisis," Staff Report no. 437, Federal Reserve Bank of New York, March 2010.

86. Gorton, "Slapped in the Face," p. 37.

87. Gorton, "Slapped in the Face," p. 37.

88. Gorton, "Slapped in the Face," p. 37.

89. Gorton, "Slapped in the Face," p. 37. Other work by Gorton argues that "we do not have anywhere near the data needed to fully understand what happened."

90. Gorton, "Slapped in the Face," p. 32. The LIBOR is a common benchmark for short-term interbank lending rates. The OIS is also used to describe the state of the interbank lending market, but it is generally the rate that financial institutions charge for an instrument that allows them to "swap" fixed-interest payments for variable-interest payments (or vice versa).

91. Gorton, "Slapped in the Face," p. 32.

92. Gorton and Metrick, "Securitized Banking and the Run on the Repo," abstract.

93. Gorton and Metrick, "Securitized Banking and the Run on the Repo," p. 10.

94. Gorton and Metrick, "Securitized Banking and the Run on the Repo," p. 11.

95. Gorton and Metrick, "Securitized Banking and the Run on the Repo," p. 13.

96. Gorton et al., "The Run on Repo and the Fed's Response," p. 1.

97. Pierre Collin-Dufresne, Robert S. Goldstein, and J. Spencer Martin, "The Determinants of Credit Spread Changes," *Journal of Finance* 56, no. 6 (December 2001): 2177–207.

98. Dennis Kuo, David Skeie, and James Vickery, "A Comparison of Libor to Other Measures of Bank Borrowing Costs," working paper, April 2018, p. 11.

99. Alex Harris, "Why It Matters That the FRA-OIS Spread Is Widening," Bloomberg, March 9, 2020. Also see Christopher Donohue and Deborah Cunningham, "Re: Comment Letter of Federated Hermes on President's Working Group Report on Money Market Mutual Funds ('MMFs') (SEC File No. S7-01-21)," letter, April 12, 2021, p. 13.

100. President's Working Group on Financial Markets, *Overview of Recent Events and Potential Reform Options for Money Market Funds*, pp. 11 and 13.

101. Hal Scott, *Connectedness and Contagion: Protecting the Financial System from Panics* (Cambridge, MA: MIT Press, 2016), p. 287. At the beginning of his book (p. 5), Scott notes that "the special feature that distinguishes contagion from other causes of systemic instability is the tendency of contagious runs

to propagate *indiscriminately, apart from connectedness.* Contagion is 'indiscriminate' when it afflicts healthy markets and solvent institutions."

102. Scott, *Connectedness and Contagion*, p. 287.

103. Scott, *Connectedness and Contagion*, p. 9.

104. Scott, *Connectedness and Contagion*, pp. 67–78.

105. Scott, *Connectedness and Contagion*, p. 67.

106. Scott, *Connectedness and Contagion*, p. 71.

107. Scott, *Connectedness and Contagion*, p. 223. Oddly, on the same page, the book also argues that "runs on such funds [prime MMFs] are unlikely to pose systemic risk concerns due to their role as funders of other financial institutions given the relatively low reliance large financial institutions have on funding from money market funds."

108. Scott, *Connectedness and Contagion*, p. 72.

109. Hugh Kim, "Contagious Runs in Money Market Funds and the Impact of a Government Guarantee," Wharton Pension Research Council Working Paper 137, October 2013, p. 4.

110. Hugh Kim, "Information Spillover of Bailouts," *Journal of Financial Intermediation*, 43 (July 2020): 1–3.

111. Gary Gorton and Andrew Metrick, "Securitized Banking and the Run on Repo," *Journal of Financial Economics* 104 (2012): 425–51.

112. Arvind Krishnamurthy, Stefan Nagel, and Dmitry Orlo, "Sizing Up Repo," *Journal of Finance* 69, no. 6 (December 2014): 2381–417. https://doi.org/10.1111/jofi.12168

113. Krishnamurthy et al., "Sizing Up Repo," pp. 2412–13.

114. Acharya et al., "Securitization without Risk Transfer," p. 522.

115. Authors' calculations using data on Table 1 (panel B) in Acharya et al., "Securitization without Risk Transfer," p. 522, and ABCP data from the Federal Reserve. See Federal Reserve Board of Governors, "Asset-Backed Commercial Paper Outstanding (ABCOMP)."

116. Scott, *Connectedness and Contagion*, p. 72.

117. Scott, *Connectedness and Contagion*, p. 73.

118. Scott, *Connectedness and Contagion*, p. 73.

119. Division of Risk, Strategy, and Financial Innovation, *Response to Questions*, p. 7.

120. Afonso et al., "Stressed, Not Frozen," p. 3. Scott also mentions that bank stock prices declined during this period because of problems in the interbank market. However, even if bank stock prices are definitively linked to isolated problems in the interbank lending market, that causal connection would not provide evidence of contagion.

Chapter 3

121. "Ownit Mortgage Solutions Goes Out of Business," *INMAN*, December 11, 2006.

122. Scott Reckard, "Demise of Ownit Mortgage Hits Home," *Los Angeles Times*, January 3, 2007.

123. Reckard, "Demise of Ownit Mortgage."

124. Jonathan Stempel, "New Century Files for Chapter 11 Bankruptcy," Reuters, April 3, 2007.

125. Stempel, "New Century Files for Chapter 11 Bankruptcy."

126. Stempel, "New Century Files for Chapter 11 Bankruptcy."

127. Julie Creswell and Vikas Bajaj, "$3.2 Billion Move by Bear Stearns to Rescue Fund," *New York Times*, June 23, 2007.

128. Creswell and Bajaj, "$3.2 Billion Move by Bear Stearns to Rescue Fund."

129. Creswell and Bajaj, "$3.2 Billion Move by Bear Stearns to Rescue Fund."

130. Gretchen Morgenson, "Inside the Countrywide Lending Spree," *New York Times*, August 26, 2007.

131. Connie Bruck, "Angelo's Ashes," *New Yorker*, June 22, 2009.

132. Bruck, "Angelo's Ashes."

133. Kimberly Amadeo, "Washington Mutual and How It Went Bankrupt," The Balance, October 12, 2021.

134. Amadeo, "Washington Mutual and How It Went Bankrupt."

135. Sudip Kar-Gupta and Yann Le Guernigou, "BNP Freezes $2.2 Bln of Funds over Subprime," Reuters, August 9, 2007.

136. Kar-Gupta and Le Guernigou, "BNP Freezes $2.2 Bln of Funds over Subprime."

137. See Hyun Song Shin, "Reflections on Northern Rock: The Bank Run That Heralded the Global Financial Crisis," *Journal of Economic Perspectives* 23, no. 1 (Winter 2009): 101–19.

138. Eric Dash, "American Home Mortgage Says It Will Close," *New York Times*, August 3, 2007.

139. Dash, "American Home Mortgage Says It Will Close."

140. Dash, "American Home Mortgage Says It Will Close."

141. Dash, "American Home Mortgage Says It Will Close." The company later filed bankruptcy. See Al Yoon, "Update 1— Accredited Home Lenders to File for Bankruptcy—Source," Reuters, May 1, 2009. The SEC later won a settlement against several American Home Mortgage executives for fraudulently misrepresenting their financial condition in "early 2007." See SEC, "SEC Charges Former American Home Mortgage Executives for Misleading Investors about Company's Financial Condition," press release, April 28, 2009.

142. Kate Stalter, "The Demise of Merrill Lynch: Revisiting Its Monumental Write-Down 10 Years Ago," *Forbes*, October 21, 2017.

143. Stalter, "The Demise of Merrill Lynch."

144. Stalter, "The Demise of Merrill Lynch."

145. Christian Plumb and Dan Wilchins, "Citi to Take $49 Bln in SIVs onto Balance Sheet," Reuters, December 13, 2007.

146. Plumb and Wilchins, "Citi to Take $49 Bln in SIVs onto Balance Sheet."

147. Dan Wilchins, "Ambac Posts $3.3 Billion Loss, but Shares Surge," Reuters, January 22, 2008.

148. Wilchins, "Ambac Posts $3.3 Billion Loss, but Shares Surge."

149. Liz Moyer, "A Decade after Its Fire-Sale Deal for Bear, a Look at What JP Morgan Got in the Bargain," CNBC, March 14, 2018.

150. Ben S. Bernanke, chairman, Board of Governors of the U.S. Federal Reserve System, Testimony on Developments in the Financial Markets, 110th Cong., 2008.

151. Louise Story, "IndyMac One of the Largest Bank Failures in U.S. History," *New York Times*, July 13, 2008.

152. Story, "IndyMac One of the Largest Bank Failures in U.S. History."

153. Federal Housing Finance Agency, "History of Fannie Mae and Freddie Mac Conservatorships," 2021.

154. Gretchen Morgenson and Louise Story, "Testy Conflict with Goldman Helped Push A.I.G. to Edge," *New York Times*, February 6, 2010.

155. Federal Reserve Board of Governors, "American International Group (AIG), Maiden Lane II and III," February 12, 2016.

156. The idea that the Fed had created the expectation of a bailout to prevent Lehman's failure is not controversial. See, for instance, John B. Taylor, "Getting Back on Track: Macroeconomic Policy Lessons from the Financial Crisis," *Federal Reserve Bank of St. Louis Review* 92, no. 3 (May/June 2010): 165–76; Alan Meltzer, "What Happened to the 'Depression'?," *Wall Street Journal*, August 31, 2009.

157. SEC, "Emergency Order Pursuant to Section 12(K) (2) of the Securities Exchange Act of 1934 Taking Temporary Action to Respond to Market Developments," Release no. 58166, July 15, 2008. Also see SEC, "SEC Enhances Investor Protections against Naked Short Selling," press release, July 15, 2008.

158. The major financial firms involved also would have known that, during the weekend of September 13, 2008, the New York Federal Reserve and the U.S. Treasury were pressuring Bank of America's chief executive officer *against* backing out of the deal to purchase Merrill Lynch. See Pratik Patel, "Bank of America's Takeover of Merrill Lynch," Case Study 147, Seven Pillars Institute, 2022.

159. Norbert J. Michel, "Lehman Brothers Bankruptcy and the Financial Crisis: Lessons Learned," Issue Brief no. 4044, Heritage Foundation, September 12, 2013.

160. Division of Risk, Strategy, and Financial Innovation, *Response to Questions*, p. 7.

161. Bureau of Economic Analysis, Gross Domestic Product (GDP), retrieved from FRED, Federal Reserve Bank of St. Louis, December 22, 2021.

162. Bureau of Labor Statistics, Unemployment Rate (UNRATE), retrieved from FRED, Federal Reserve Bank of St. Louis, December 21, 2021.

163. Bureau of Labor Statistics, Employment Level (CE16OV), retrieved from FRED, Federal Reserve Bank of St. Louis, December 22, 2021.

164. S&P Dow Jones Indices LLC, S&P/Case-Shiller U.S. National Home Price Index (CSUSHPINSA), retrieved from FRED, Federal Reserve Bank of St. Louis, December 21, 2021.

165. Sharon L. Crenson and Kathleen M. Howley, "U.S. Subprime Mortgage Delinquencies at 4-Year High (Update 3)," Bloomberg, March 13, 2007. Also see Michel, "Lehman Brothers Bankruptcy and the Financial Crisis."

166. Atif Mian and Amir Sufi, "What Explains the 2007–2009 Drop in Employment?" *Econometrica* 82, no. 6 (November 2014): 2197–223.

167. Mian and Sufi, "What Explains the 2007–2009 Drop in Employment?," p. 2211. Also see Lawrence Summers, "Lawrence Summers on 'House of Debt,'" *Financial Times*, June 6, 2014.

Chapter 4

168. Hal Scott, for instance, refers to the success of the federal programs launched during the 2008 crisis and argues that the only options to stop contagion "are: (1) prohibit prime funds, retail or institutional; (2) insure prime funds in some manner; or, (3) provide strong lender of last resort to such funds." See Scott, *Connectedness and Contagion*, p. 230.

169. Government Accountability Office, *Federal Reserve Bank Governance: Opportunities Exist to Broaden Director Recruitment Efforts and Increase Transparency*, Report to Congressional Addressees, GAO-12-18 (Washington: GAO, October 2011), p. 94.

170. Government Accountability Office, *Federal Reserve System: Opportunities Exist to Strengthen Policies and Processes for Managing Emergency Assistance*, Report to Congressional Addressees, GAO–11–696 (Washington: GAO, July 2011), p. 131.

171. For a complete list and additional details, see Government Accountability Office, *Federal Reserve Bank Governance: Opportunities Exist to Broaden Director Recruitment Efforts and Increase Transparency*, p. 76. See also Lawrence H. White, Testimony before the Subcommittee on Monetary Policy and Trade, Committee on Financial Services, U.S. House of Representatives, March 12, 2014; and Michel, "The Fed's Failure as a Lender of Last Resort."

172. Author's calculations using Federal Reserve data available at Federal Reserve Board of Governors, "Term Auction Facility (TAF)," February 12, 2016.

173. Michael J. Fleming and Nicholas J. Klagge, "The Federal Reserve's Foreign Exchange Swap Lines," Federal Reserve Bank of New York, *Current Issues in Economics and Finance* 16, no. 4 (April 2010): 4.

174. Fleming and Klagge, "The Federal Reserve's Foreign Exchange Swap Lines," p. 5.

175. Federal Reserve Board of Governors, "Term Securities Lending Facility," February 5, 2010.

176. Federal Reserve Board of Governors, "Term Securities Lending Facility."

177. Author's calculations using Federal Reserve data available at Federal Reserve Board of Governors, "Term Securities Lending Facility (TSLF) and TSLF Options Program (TOP)," February 12, 2016. These amounts do not include securities loaned through TOP.

178. Author's calculations using Federal Reserve data available at Federal Reserve Board of Governors, "Primary Dealer Credit Facility (PDCF)," March 18, 2020. The data provided do not include lending in the month of August.

179. Brian Sheridan, "Lender of Last Resort: An Examination of the Federal Reserve's Primary Dealer Credit Facility," working paper, University of Notre Dame, April 2011, p. 29.

180. After the Lehman failure, 26.4 percent of the collateral consisted of equity securities and 16 percent consisted of speculative-grade bonds. See Sheridan, "Lender of Last Resort," p. 16.

181. Author's calculations using Federal Reserve data available at Federal Reserve Board of Governors, "Asset-Backed Commercial Paper Money Market Mutual Fund Liquidity Facility (AMLF)," March 20, 2020.

182. Federal Reserve Board of Governors, "Commercial Paper Funding Facility (CPFF)," March 18, 2020.

183. Author's calculations using Federal Reserve data available at Federal Reserve Board of Governors, "Commercial Paper Funding Facility (CPFF)."

184. Adam Ashcraft, Allan Malz, and Zoltan Pozsar, "The Federal Reserve's Term Asset-Backed Securities Loan Facility," *Federal Reserve Bank of New York Economic Policy Review* (November 2012): 29.

185. Federal Reserve Bank of New York, "New York Fed 101: Term Asset-Backed Securities Loan Facility (TALF)," June 2011.

186. Federal Reserve Bank of New York, "New York Fed 101."

187. QE2 was initiated in November 2010 and was designed to purchase $75 billion per month of longer-termed Treasuries, for a total of $600 billion. See Norbert Michel and Stephen Moore, "Quantitative Easing, the Fed's Balance Sheet, and Central Bank Insolvency," Backgrounder no. 2938, Heritage Foundation, August 14, 2014.

188. U.S. Department of the Treasury, "Treasury Announces Temporary Guarantee Program for Money Market Funds," September 29, 2008. Treasury did not allow MMFs that had suspended redemptions or broken the buck to apply; any participant whose net asset value dropped below $0.995 per share was forced to liquidate its assets. According to Treasury, the program incurred no losses. See Department of the Treasury, "Treasury Announces Expiration of Guarantee Program for Money Market Funds," September 18, 2009. Also see Martha L. Cochran, David F. Freeman, and Helen Mayer Clark, "Money Market Fund Reform: SEC Rulemaking in the FSOC Era," *Columbia Business Law Review* 2015, no. 3 (February 16, 2016): 861–966.

189. In July 2010, the Dodd-Frank Act made the increase to $250,000 permanent. Mark Calabria, "Rethinking Title III: The Federal Deposit Insurance Corporation and Other Subtitles," in *The Case Against Dodd–Frank: How the "Consumer Protection" Law Endangers Americans*, ed. Norbert J. Michel, pp. 87–91 (Washington: Heritage Foundation, 2016).

190. The FDIC adopted its final rule for the TLGP on November 21, 2008. The TLGP was established after "a determination of systemic risk by the Secretary of the Treasury (after consultation with the President), following receipt of the written recommendation of the Board on October 13, 2008, along with a similar written recommendation of the Board of Governors of the Federal Reserve System (FRB)," all in accordance with "section 13(c)(4)(G) to the Federal Deposit Insurance Act (FDI Act), 12 U.S.C. 1823(c)(4)(G)." See Federal Deposit Insurance Corporation, "Temporary Liquidity Guarantee Program," Final Rule, *Federal Register* 73, no. 229 (November 26, 2008): 72244–73.

191. Norbert J. Michel, "Dodd-Frank's Title XI Does Not End Federal Reserve Bailouts," Backgrounder no. 3060, Heritage Foundation, September 29, 2015, pp. 10–11.

192. Calabria, "Rethinking Title III: The Federal Deposit Insurance Corporation and Other Subtitles."

193. Scott, *Connectedness and Contagion*, p. 78.

194. FSOC, "Proposed Recommendations," p. 26.

195. From a regulatory standpoint, regulators from the same government backing the securities would have to attest to the value and safety of those securities, so there is no inherent reason that financial institutions should fear holding them on their balance sheets. And, in fact, multiple government reports document the flow of money into the government sector (often referred to as a *flight to quality*).

196. News accounts confirm that retail customers with insured balances ran to get their money out of Washington Mutual and IndyMac. See Andrea Chang, E. Scott Reckard, and Kathy Kristof, "Confusion at IndyMac Fuels Customers' Anger," *Los Angeles Times*, July 16, 2008; Joe Weisenthal, "There Really Was a Massive Run on WaMu," *Business Insider*, October 29, 2009; and

Lending Tree, "Two-Year Anniversary of WaMu's Closure—A Look Back from a Depositor's Point of View," *Deposit Accounts* (blog), September 25, 2010.

Chapter 5

197. Anderson and Gascon, "The Commercial Paper Market" p. 603.

198. The outstanding ABCP share of total commercial paper outstanding steadily increased from 49 percent in 2004 to 58 percent in June 2007. Author's calculations using the following data series: Federal Reserve Board of Governors, Asset-Backed Commercial Paper Outstanding (ABCOMP), retrieved from FRED, Federal Reserve Bank of St. Louis, December 27, 2021; and Federal Reserve Board of Governors, Commercial Paper Outstanding (COMPOUT), retrieved from FRED, Federal Reserve Bank of St. Louis, December 27, 2021.

199. For instance, one proponent of the conventional story writes that a "major element [of the crisis] was the lack of sufficient oversight and regulation of large, complex, and interconnected shadow banks and risky activities that emerged outside of the core banking sector." See Gregg Gelzinis, "Strengthening the Regulation and Oversight of Shadow Banks," Fact Sheet, Center for American Progress, July 18, 2019.

200. Gorton and Metrick, "Securitized Banking and the Run on Repo," p. 430.

201. Gorton and Metrick, "Securitized Banking and the Run on Repo," p. 432.

202. Gorton and Metrick, "Regulating the Shadow Banking System," pp. 277–78.

203. See Norbert J. Michel, "Fixing the Regulatory Framework for Derivatives," Backgrounder no. 3156, Heritage Foundation, September 14, 2016. Also see Mark Roe, "The Derivatives Market's Payment Priorities as Financial Crisis Accelerator," *Stanford Law Review* 63 (2011): 552. Specifically, Roe notes that "Congress added derivatives priorities to the Code over the last three decades, expanding them in 1982, 1984, 1994, 2005, and 2006."

204. Michel, "Fixing the Regulatory Framework for Derivatives," pp. 7–8.

205. Had repos been treated as secure loans without the safe harbors, it is also unlikely that Lehman could have conducted the Repo 105 transaction, further obscuring the company's true leverage. Michel, "Fixing the Regulatory Framework for Derivatives," p. 9.

206. Michel, "Fixing the Regulatory Framework for Derivatives," p. 9. It is also noteworthy that CDSs and even synthetic CDOs were created by employees of J. P. Morgan, one of the nation's oldest and largest commercial banks. At least as early as 1991, federal regulators were considering new regulations for these derivative securities, and the New York Fed president, E. Gerald Corrigan, had personally contacted J. P. Morgan's CEO to discuss the bank's derivatives business. Tett, *Fool's Gold*, p. 23.

207. Roe, "The Derivatives Market's Payment Priorities as Financial Crisis Accelerator," p. 552.

208. Roe, "The Derivatives Market's Payment Priorities as Financial Crisis Accelerator," p. 552.

209. Federal Reserve Board, "Agencies Issue Final Rule on Capital Requirements for Asset-Backed Commercial Paper Programs," joint press release, July 20, 2004.

210. Office of the Comptroller of the Currency, Treasury; Federal Reserve Board of Governors; Federal Deposit Insurance Corporation; and Office of Thrift Supervision, Treasury, "Risk-Based Capital Guidelines; Capital Adequacy Guidelines; Capital Maintenance: Consolidation of Asset-Backed Commercial Paper Programs and Other Related Issues," Final Rule, p. 4. For a general description of the interaction between FASB and federal banking regulators, see Acharya et al., "Securitization without Risk Transfer," p. 524.

211. In fact, Stephen Partridge-Hicks and Nicholas Sossidis, employees of Citibank, created the SIV concept explicitly to exploit the Basel capital rules and lower the bank's capital charge. It is not possible for a commercial bank to engage in this type of capital charge alteration without the unambiguous blessing of federal regulators. Tett, *Fool's Gold*, p. 97.

212. For more on this ABCP innovation that started in the 1990s, see Anderson and Gascon, "The Commercial Paper Market," pp. 599–602, and Acharya et al., "Securitization without Risk Transfer."

213. Acharya et al., "Securitization without Risk Transfer," Table 2, p. 523.

214. For more on the risk bucket approach, see Howard D. Crosse, *Management Policies for Commercial Banks* (Englewood Cliffs, NJ: Prentice Hall, 1962), pp. 169–72. The later amendment regarding the lower weight for highly rated private-label mortgage securities was known as the recourse rule. See Jeffrey Friedman and Wladimir Kraus, *Engineering the Financial Crisis: Systemic Risk and the Failure of Regulation* (Philadelphia: University of Pennsylvania Press, 2011), p. 69.

215. Friedman and Kraus, *Engineering the Financial Crisis*, p. 81.

216. Norbert J. Michel and John L. Ligon, "Basel III Capital Standards Do Not Reduce the Too-Big-to-Fail Problem," Backgrounder no. 2905, Heritage Foundation, April 23, 2014.

217. Charles W. Calomiris and Stephen H. Haber, *Fragile by Design: The Political Origins of Banking Crises and Scarce Credit* (Princeton, NJ: Princeton University Press, 2014), p. ix.

218. Calomiris and Haber, *Fragile by Design*, p. 3.

219. Calomiris and Haber, *Fragile by Design*, p. 4.

220. Calomiris and Haber, *Fragile by Design*, pp. 6–7.

221. While it may be tempting to argue that banking—or a market economy itself—is inherently unstable, the record shows that financial crises are not inherent to market economies or to the production of bank debt. In general, market economies other than the United States have performed with fewer banking crises, and most U.S. crises have been directly linked to poorly designed banking and currency regulations. See George Selgin, "Misunderstanding Financial History," *Alt-M*, July 11, 2013.

222. For the sake of completeness, it is also untrue that financial markets were deregulated in any significant way leading up to the 2008 crisis or that federal regulators simply erred by failing to consider systemic risks in financial markets. See Norbert J. Michel,

"The Myth of Financial Market Deregulation," Backgrounder no. 3094, Heritage Foundation, April 26, 2016; and Norbert J. Michel, "Step One for Improving Financial Institution Supervision: Ending the Federal Reserve's Regulatory Role," testimony before the Subcommittee on Financial Institutions and Consumer Protection of the Senate Committee on Banking, Housing and Urban Affairs, November 21, 2014. Also see a 1996 speech by Federal Reserve Chairman Alan Greenspan claiming that "a central mission of the Federal Reserve" is "to maintain financial stability and reduce and contain systemic risks." Alan Greenspan, remarks/ speech, Annual Dinner and Francis Boyer Lecture, American Enterprise Institute for Public Policy Research, Washington, December 5, 1996.

Chapter 6

223. Karen Arenson, "Volcker Proposes Money Funds Be Subject to Rules on Reserves," *New York Times*, June 26, 1981.

224. Karen Arenson, "Volcker Proposes Money Funds Be Subject to Rules on Reserves."

225. Reuters staff, "Volcker: Money Funds Weaken Financial System," Reuters, August 25, 2009. For a different perspective, that is, that MMFs reduce systemic risks, see Jonathan Macey, "Reducing Systemic Risk: The Role of Money Market Mutual Funds as Substitutes for Federally Insured Bank Deposits," SEC Comment, January 2011.

226. FSOC, "Proposed Recommendations," pp. 29-61.

227. President's Working Group on Financial Markets, *Money Market Fund Reform Options*, p. 8.

228. President's Working Group on Financial Markets, *Money Market Fund Reform Options*, p. 8.

229. McCabe, "The Cross Section of Money Market Fund Risks and Financial Crises," p. 1.

230. Investment Company Institute, *2009 Investment Company Fact Book: A Review of Trends and Activities in the Investment Company Industry* (Washington: Investment Company Institute, 2009) p. 146.

231. U.S. Securities and Exchange Commission, "Reserve Primary Fund Distributes Assets to Investors," press release, January 29, 2010.

232. See U.S. Department of the Treasury, "Treasury Announces Temporary Guarantee Program for Money Market Funds"; U.S. Department of the Treasury, "Treasury Announces Expiration of Guarantee Program for Money Market Funds"; and Shefali Anand, "Treasury Pads Coffers in Bailout," *Wall Street Journal*, February 17, 2009. Anand reports that "one reason for the success of the money-fund bailout is that the problems were relatively simple and contained. Money funds held high-quality and short-term assets, so the risk of guaranteeing them wasn't high for the government."

233. These figures are approximated by using information in the following report: Sean Hoskins, "An Overview of the Transaction Account Guarantee (TAG) Program and the Potential Impact of Its Expiration or Extension," Congressional Research Service R42787, November 27, 2012, pp. 10–11.

234. Federal Deposit Insurance Corporation, "Bank Failures & Assistance Data," December 28, 2021.

235. They also argue that sponsor support may have obscured investors' appreciation for how risky MMFs really were, but given that investors did not lose money, it is difficult to agree with such a claim. FSOC, "Proposed Recommendations," p. 20. The report states, "Unlike other types of mutual funds, MMF sponsors have often supported their funds, with researchers documenting over 200 instances of such support since 1989."

236. Although it does not empirically test the hypothesis, one academic paper posits that "even though fund sponsors have no contractual obligation to support their funds, they may find it optimal to do so, because the costs of not providing support may be large. Such costs are typically reputational in nature, in that an individual fund's default could generate outflows from other mutual funds managed by the same sponsor, or a loss of the sponsor's general business." See Marcin Kacperczyk and Philipp Schnabl, "How Safe Are Money Market Funds?" *Quarterly Journal of Economics* 128, no. 3 (August 2013): 1082. https://doi .org/10.1093/qje/qjt010 Separately, the SEC acknowledges that

it is incorrect to assume that funds receiving (or seeking) sponsor support would necessarily have broken the buck had they not received (or sought) sponsor support. See Division of Risk, Strategy, and Financial Innovation, *Response to Questions*, p. 17.

237. For more detail on how MMFs are structured, see Hester Peirce and Robert Greene, "Opening the Gate to Money Market Fund Reform," *Pace Law Review* 34, no. 3 (July 2014). For a complete list of rule changes prior to 2010, see Investment Company Institute, *Report of the Money Market Working Group*, pp. 141–66.

238. Investment Company Institute, *Report of the Money Market Working Group*, pp. 150–51. The average portfolio maturity was dollar-weighted average.

239. Investment Company Institute, *Report of the Money Market Working Group*, p. 150.

240. Cochran et al., "Money Market Fund Reform," pp. 879-80.

241. Peirce and Greene, "Opening the Gate to Money Market Fund Reform," p. 1097.

242. SEC, "Money Market Fund Reforms."

243. See Division of Risk, Strategy, and Financial Innovation, *Response to Questions*, p. 18.

244. SEC, "SEC Approves Money Market Fund Reforms to Better Protect Investors," press release, January 27, 2010.

245. SEC, "SEC Approves Money Market Fund Reforms to Better Protect Investors."

246. Peirce and Greene, "Opening the Gate to Money Market Fund Reform," p. 1125.

247. Investment Company Institute, *2019 Investment Company Factbook: A Review of Trends and Activities in the Investment Company Industry* (Washington: Investment Company Institute, 2019), p. 232.

248. SEC, "Money Market Fund Reform; Amendments to Form PF," Final Rule, 17 CFR parts 230, 239, 270, 274, and 279, July 23, 2014. Also see SEC, "SEC Adopts Money Market Fund Reform Rules," press release, July 23, 2014.

249. Jeffrey N. Gordon and Christopher M. Gandia, "Money Market Funds Run Risk: Will Floating Net Asset Value Fix the Problem?," *Columbia Business Law Review* 2014, no. 2 (August 6, 2014): 314–70. https://doi.org/10.7916/cblr.v2014i2.1775

250. Investment Company Institute, *2017 Investment Company Factbook: A Review of Trends and Activities in the Investment Company Industry* (Washington: Investment Company Institute, 2017), p. 51. Also see Donohue and Cunningham, "Re: Comment Letter of Federated Hermes."

251. Investment Company Institute, *2017 Investment Company Factbook*, p. 53.

252. SEC, "Money Market Fund Reforms."

253. SEC, "Statement on Proposed Amendments to Money Market Fund Rules," Commissioner Caroline A. Crenshaw, December 15, 2021.

254. SEC, "Statement on Money Market Fund Reforms," Commissioner Hester Peirce, December 15, 2021.

255. The SEC actually authorized the use of swing pricing in 2018, though the agency did not require it. For more on swing pricing, see Anil Kashyap, Donald Kohn, and David Wessel, "What Is Swing Pricing?," *Up Front*, Brookings Institution, August 3, 2021; BlackRock, "Swing Pricing–Raising the Bar," *Policy Spotlight*, September 2021; Dunhong Jin et al., "Swing Pricing and Fragility in Open-End Mutual Funds," IMF Working Paper 2019, no. 227, International Monetary Fund, November 2019; https://doi.org/10.5089/9781513518336.001 and Ulf Lewrick and Jochen Schanz, "Is the Price Right? Swing Pricing and Investor Redemptions," BIS Working Paper no. 664, Bank for International Settlements, October 11, 2017.

256. 17 CFR §270.2a-7(a) and 17 CFR §270.2a-7(28).

257. President's Working Group on Financial Markets, *Overview of Recent Events and Potential Reform Options for Money Market Funds*, pp. 11–12.

258. Board of Governors of the Federal Reserve System, "Federal Reserve Board Broadens Program of Support for the Flow of Credit to Households and Businesses by Establishing a Money Market Mutual Fund Liquidity Facility (MMLF)," press release, March 18, 2020.

259. Shelly Antoniewicz, "On Closer Look, a Very Different Picture of Funds' Role in the Commercial Paper Market," *Viewpoints*, Investment Company Institute, April 21, 2021.

260. Larry White, "Recent Trouble among Money-Market Mutual Funds, and the Way Forward," *Alt-M*, March 31, 2020.

Chapter 7

261. For instance, Senator Dianne Feinstein (D-CA), who is not on the Senate Banking Committee, introduced a bill to reduce climate change through financial regulation. See Senator Dianne Feinstein, "Bill to Reduce Climate Change Risk in Financial System Draws Broad Support," press release, March 11, 2021. Jamie Dimon, the CEO of JPMorgan Chase, is just one example of an industry participant who supports extensive federal regulation. As the *Wall Street Journal* reports, Dimon recently "highlighted the benefits of a safer and stronger banking system because of higher capital, liquidity, more disclosure and transparency, and stress testing, among other changes." See Emily Glazer, "Jamie Dimon Pushes for Simpler, More Coordinated Bank Regulations," *Wall Street Journal*, April 4, 2017.

262. See, for example, Glenn Hubbard et al., *Report of the Task Force on Financial Stability*, (Chicago: Hutchins Center, Brookings Institution, June 2021).

263. Hubbard et al., *Report of the Task Force on Financial Stability*, pp. 7–8.

264. SEC, "Money Market Fund Reforms," p. 172.

265. Brian Begalle et al., "The Risk of Fire Sales in the Tri-Party Repo Market," Federal Reserve Bank of New York Staff Report no. 616, May 2013, p. 1.

266. This section ignores the fact that the concept of *financial stability* is difficult to objectively define and that Congress chose to leave the term undefined in the Dodd-Frank Act, despite giving federal regulators a mandate to "to identify risks to the financial stability of the United States that could arise from the material financial distress or failure, or ongoing activities, of large, interconnected bank holding companies or nonbank financial companies, or that could arise outside the financial services marketplace." See 12 U.S.C. §5322.

267. Begalle et al., "The Risk of Fire Sales in the Tri-Party Repo Market," p. 9.

268. Begalle et al., "The Risk of Fire Sales in the Tri-Party Repo Market," p. 10.

269. Begalle et al., "The Risk of Fire Sales in the Tri-Party Repo Market," p. 6.

270. Craig B. Merrill et al., "Did Capital Requirements and Fair Value Accounting Spark Fire Sales in Distressed Mortgage-Backed Securities?" National Bureau of Economic Research Working Paper no. 18270, August 2012, p. 2.

271. Merrill et al., "Did Capital Requirements and Fair Value Accounting Spark Fire Sales in Distressed Mortgage-Backed Securities?," p. 31.

272. Alberto Manconi, Massimo Massa, and Ayako Yasuda, "The Role of Institutional Investors in Propagating the Crisis of 2007–2008," *Journal of Financial Economics* 104, no. 3 (June 2012): 2. https://doi.org/10.1016/j.jfineco.2011.05.011

273. Manconi et al., "The Role of Institutional Investors in Propagating the Crisis of 2007–2008," p. 32.

274. See, for example, Stephen G. Cecchetti and Kermit L. Schoenholtz, "The Urgent Agenda for Financial Reform," *Money and Banking* (blog), October 4, 2021.

275. Saule T. Omarova, "From Gramm-Leach-Bliley to Dodd-Frank: The Unfulfilled Promise of Section 23A of the Federal Reserve Act," *North Carolina Law Review* 89, no. 5 (June 2011): 1775.

276. Omarova, "From Gramm-Leach-Bliley to Dodd-Frank," 1686.

277. Technically, the FDIC regulates only FDIC-insured non-Fed member state-chartered banks, but that category effectively includes all commercial banks. See Norbert J. Michel and David R. Burton, "Financial Institutions: Necessary for Prosperity," Backgrounder no. 3108, Heritage Foundation, April 14, 2016.

278. Private deposit insurance could replace FDIC insurance, and the FDIC's insurance limits could be drastically reduced given the size of the average transaction and savings account balances. Globally, several market-based options (such as the one used in New Zealand) could replace the FDIC's bank resolution process, bringing much-needed market discipline to the banking industry. See Michel and Burton, "Financial Institutions: Necessary for Prosperity," p. 12.

ABOUT THE AUTHOR

Norbert J. Michel is vice president and director of the Cato Institute's Center for Monetary and Financial Alternatives, where he specializes in issues pertaining to financial markets and monetary policy. Michel was most recently the Director for Data Analysis at the Heritage Foundation, where he edited and contributed chapters to two books: *The Case Against Dodd–Frank: How the "Consumer Protection" Law Endangers Americans* and *Prosperity Unleashed: Smarter Financial Regulation.*

Michel was previously a tenured professor at Nicholls State University's College of Business, teaching finance, economics, and statistics. Before that, he worked at Heritage as a tax policy analyst in the think tank's Center for Data Analysis from 2002 to 2005. He previously was with the global energy company Entergy, where he worked on models to help predict bankruptcies of commercial clients.

Michel holds a doctoral degree in financial economics from the University of New Orleans. He received his bachelor of business administration degree in finance and economics from Loyola University. He currently resides in Virginia.

ABOUT THE CATO INSTITUTE AND CENTER FOR MONETARY AND FINANCIAL ALTERNATIVES

Founded in 1977, the Cato Institute is a public policy research foundation dedicated to broadening the parameters of policy debate to allow consideration of more options that are consistent with the principles of limited government, individual liberty, and peace. The Institute is named for *Cato's Letters*, libertarian pamphlets that were widely read in the American colonies in the early 18th century and played a major role in laying the philosophical foundation for the American Revolution.

The Cato Institute undertakes an extensive publications program on the complete spectrum of policy issues. Books, monographs, and shorter studies are commissioned to examine the federal budget, Social Security, regulation, military spending, international trade, and myriad other issues. Major policy conferences are held throughout the year.

The Cato Institute's Center for Monetary and Financial Alternatives was founded in 2014 to assess the shortcomings of existing monetary and financial regulatory arrangements, and to discover and promote more stable and efficient alternatives.

In order to maintain its independence, the Cato Institute accepts no government funding. Contributions are received from foundations, corporations, and individuals, and other revenue is generated from the sale of publications. The Institute is a nonprofit, tax-exempt, educational foundation under Section 501(c)3 of the Internal Revenue Code.

CATO INSTITUTE
1000 Massachusetts Ave. NW
Washington, DC 20001
www.cato.org